MW00352123

This book is about the universal tr⟨...⟩ Mary Jo tries to solve her mom w⟨...⟩ ⟨...⟩ drawers and boxes. Learning about Mary Jo's mom helped me understand my own. I loved it.—Laurie Kilmartin, *Dead People Suck*

Dumb Dumb Dumb gives the reader an insight into Mary Jo Pehl's remarkable mother-a woman of many contradictions. A voracious reader who kept ratings and synopses of everything she read. A taste for the pragmatic and macabre, she doesn't suffer romance and I found that delightful. Also, an interesting category of hoarder. Get ready to take notes when you read this book. It offers so much in the way of attitudes towards life and a kick ass reading list not to mention many laugh out loud moments seen thru Ms. Pehl's endearing wit.—Laraine Newman, Founding member of The Groundlings and OG SNL

Let's face it. Everybody's mother is a piece of work. But in this often hilarious book, Mary Jo Pehl has done the impossible: figured out a way to honor her mother's tireless efforts as a compulsive reader by creating a portrait of her using the hundreds of short and often terse book reviews she left behind. When combined with the carefully observed and lovingly crafted anecdotes written by a devoted daughter who was also a fan, Mary Jo manages to bring her family to life as a group of folks who are fun to hang out with.—Merrill Markoe, Humorist, *We Saw Scenery*

This book cracked me open. Read it with a baguette, a box of Kleenex, and your mom on speed dial.—Cate Berry, *Penguin & Tiny Shrimp Don't Do Bedtime* and *Chicken Break-A Counting Book.*

Poignant and laugh-out-loud funny. A quest for understanding memories catalyzed when Mary Jo Pehl discovers her deceased mother's hand-written book reviews. A wonderful read. —Matt Goldman, NYT Best Selling Author of *Carolina Moonset*

In this endearing and hilarious memoir, Mary Jo Pehl celebrates the relationship she shared with her quirky, wise and opinionated mother. It's about love and loss and how humor enriches both. *Dumb Dumb Dumb* is funny, funny, funny; tender, tender, tender, and a joy, joy, joy to read.—Lorna Landvik, *Chronicles Of A Radical Hag (With Recipes)*

Through her mother's hilariously terse book reviews, Mary Jo finds a funny and touching kaleidoscope of memories, emotions, and life. —Elliot Kalan, *The Flop House Podcast*; writer, *Maniac of New York*; former head writer, *The Daily Show with John Stewart*

A funny and touching look at how we all turn into our parents, in one way or another, and how everybody's a critic, whether or not we exhaustively use a note-card system. Mary Jo Pehl has always been hilarious, but now she reveals her heartfelt side as well. —Alonso Duralde, *Have Yourself a Movie Little Christmas*, Linoleum Knife podcast, *The Wrap*

Dumb
Dumb
Dumb

My Mother's Book Reviews

Mary Jo Pehl

REDHAWK
PUBLICATIONS

Redhawk Publications
The Catawba Valley Community College Press
2550 US Hwy 70 SE
Hickory NC 28602

ISBN: 978-1-952485-41-1

Library of Congress Control Number: 2021947351

Printed in the United States of America

First Printing
First Edition

If this book is autographed, it is from the first 200 copies of the first printing, first edition.

For my fellow wolves

My mother possessed what she liked to call "the Cadillac of tweezers."

Forged in brushed nickel, the tips were beveled to such a fine point they were practically a surgical instrument for the small bristly hairs that sprung up on her chin. My mother liked to faux-casually name-drop the manufacturer like it was a close personal friend: *Wusthof.*

The tweezers were always within arm's reach of her recliner, where she read for hours every day. At an angle the better part of each day, she'd be tilted back, a book in her lap and a pair of whimsically-colored reading glasses on a chain around her neck, a glass of water, a magnifying mirror, and a stack of books on the cabinet next to the chair.

Most of my adult life, I would stop by my parents' house once a week or so, just to say hi or score a meal or pick up mail that still occasionally got delivered to their house. I hadn't lived with them for decades, but they always saved my mail, even the junk mail - *just in case it might be important,* they'd say. My mother would take a break from her reading and set the book down on her lap as I sat across from her in the matching recliner. She was short and her legs barely reached the footrest, and at that slant, I was looking up her nostrils more than straight in the eyes.

We'd talk. Machinery in my father's woodshop hummed through the floor as he worked on some project downstairs. My mother and I talked about my siblings and the grandchildren. We talked about friends: mine and hers. My love life or lack thereof. My job or lack thereof. Movies and television. Food. Diets. Recipes, always low-calorie.

And books, always books, whatever each of us was reading at the time. She'd describe the book that was currently splayed on her plush lap, all the while running her fingers along her chin in search of goat hairs that might have sprung up. Looking over her reading glasses at me, she'd slap the palm of her hand on the cover and declare, "But I could swear I've read the damn thing before.

"Honest to Pete, I can't remember what I've read anymore."

A few months after my mother died, my father and I sorted through three large closets, gorged with stuff she'd found at Goodwill, garage sales, or consignment stores over the years. She loved to shop. There were clothes with price tags still attached, saved for the day she would lose the appropriate amount of weight and they would fit. Other clothes had once fit and were saved for the day they would fit again. There were kitchen gadgets and utensils, books, games and puzzles, crockpots, heating pads, all stashed away for birthdays or Christmas and labeled with the intended recipient's name. A Halloween snow globe had a post-it note stuck to it with my husband's name scrawled on it. The globe was the head of Frankenstein's monster, and it rained a "snow" of black particles when you shook it. I set it aside and we bagged up everything else for Goodwill, a sort of mercantile "circle of life." My once-tall father reached on tiptoes for a clear plastic recipe box on the top shelf and we clicked open the lid. It was full of index cards with my mother's notes on all the books she'd read the past fifteen-plus years.

She read so many books she had to start keeping track.

Brass Verdict
Michael Connelly
Can't remember but kept me interested.

Coffin Dancer
Deaver
Can't remember.

[?]
Forgot name but was good
Stephen Cannell

The Closers
Michael Connelly
Can't remember but enjoyed it.

Laws of Our Father
Turow, Scott
Got long + a bit boring. Can't remember plot.

Fuzz
McBain, Ed
(No rating)
Didn't finish + can't remember what it was about – got involved in another book.

[?]
Patterson, James
Read but can't remember the name – but did enjoy.

Crais, Robert   ?
La Requem
       Can't remember but know
I read it

For such a small box it was hefty in my hands. "You keep it," my father said as he tied up one of the many trash bags. "You're the writer in the family, after all."

Almost a year later, I sat in a coffee shop with a notebook, a pen, and the box. I smoothed all the cards over and over again as they lay on the table in front of me, like a blackjack dealer sweeping up after a hand. The 400-plus cards were mostly alphabetized by the author's last name, but some were out of order, so I put them back in place. My mother wrote the book's title in the upper left-hand corner and under that, the author. The month and year she read them are in the upper right hand corner. The earliest one is from 1997. She ranked most of the books on a scale of 0-10, and in the body of the card are plot summaries or thoughts on the book, pithy one- or two-sentence reviews. In her squat, looping cursive, the sentences sometimes straggle past the light blue lines on the cards and dip downward, maybe from balancing them on her lap as she wrote in her recliner.

I read and reread all the cards. Who was this woman I'd known my whole life? This woman I *thought* I knew? How could I, who had won several spelling bees in elementary school, be the progeny of someone who misspelled a major country?

Daughter of Fortune
Isabel Allende
7/10
Girl from Chili gets to America Gold rush.
Chinese man.
Romance and adventure

How could I - who considered the *AP Style Manual* and *The Elements of Style* summer beach reads - have possibly been borne of the loins of someone who used greengrocer apostrophes?

Louisiana Power and Light
John Dufresne
6/10
Downer of a book about a family (Fontana's)
who seem to have a curse on them for many generations.

How could I, who had read *Moby-Dick* twice, be the issue of a woman who freely admitted, in writing no less, to reading schlockmeister Sidney Sheldon?

Sky Is Falling
Sheldon, Sidney
6/10
So-so book about female (beautiful) newsreader looking into the deaths
of wealthy family of 5 - all are accidents and within one year.

Some of the cards are missing titles, so I do a little sleuthing. Others need deciphering because of my mother's scrawl, or there are incomplete sentences or misspellings. I've transcribed the entries as she wrote them, as best I can deduce from my mother's handwriting, and filling in the blanks where I could. Some clarifications are in brackets. There are references to events I don't remember, and comments I wish I could ask her about.

True Story of Kelly Gang
Pete Carey
Got about half way and ruined book with water spill in athletic bag.
Australian gang of dirt poor Irish - may finish later.

Skin Tight
Hiaason, Carl
Can't remember much as I read it while in hospital.

Protect + Defend
Patterson, Richard North
8/10
Abortion, Supreme Court + nasty politics. Sometimes painful.

[My] Sisters Keeper
Picoult, Jodi
Mind blowing.

Altar Music
Weber, Christine (sic) Lore
Religious life in convents of 40s+ 50s.
Probably close to the truth but made me uncomfortable.

[The Book Thief]
Zusak, Markus
Narrator is dead. 2nd World War. Young girl in Nazi Germany.
Left me with much to think about.

They're all tiny snapshots, pieces of a photomosaic just waiting to happen. Maybe all I need to do is assemble them just right so I can truly see my mother.

The last words I spoke to my mother were about cheesecake.

My sister had called me: *You need to get home. Now.* I got the last flight from Austin to Minneapolis on a Sunday night and got to the hospital close to midnight. My sisters and brothers were crowded into the hospital room and my father raised his arms like he was going to hug me when I walked into the room. But my mother's bed was between us and he sat down again as if pulled back by his bewilderment. The sheets and blankets were pulled up smooth and neat under her arms. She hadn't moved to muss the bedding. I leaned over and put my cheek against hers, my belly getting pinched on the metal bed rail. She'd given me her wedding ring when I got married, and I slipped it back on her finger. Even after a year of chemo and radiation, my mother's cheeks were still cool and velvety.

"I ate the cheesecake, Mom."

Her face seemed to turn toward me. All I could think was that my breath must be stinky from airline food and the long flight, and she would leave this earth with that last sensory experience. I looked at her so hard my eyeballs started to hurt. My mother never quite knew how beautiful she was, with her high cheekbones, tawny skin, a graceful streamlined nose, and full lips over front teeth that she was always self-conscious about. As a kid, I loved to watch her get ready for a rare evening out. After a spritz of *Jean Naté* and pinning in a wiglet to make her hair poofy, she'd lean into the enormous bathroom mirror to put on lipstick, a deep red lustrous against her olive skin and black hair. She'd rub her front teeth with her forefinger to clean off any lipstick that might have smeared on them.

"I ate the cheesecake. I'm sorry. I'm sorry, Mom, I'm so sorry." Of everything that went through my mind on the flight to Minnesota, I hadn't once even thought about *the cheesecake*. She'd probably been waiting her whole life to win this argument.

Charms for the Easy Life
Gibbons, Kaye
7/10
Daughter, mother, grandmother relationship. 1930's & 40's. Midwifery and general healing.

The Bonesetter's Daughter
Tan, Amy
8/10
Almost as good as her other books –
another mother-daughter relationship but love the way she writes.

It was the night before Thanksgiving and my mother had already made the potatoes and stuffing for the next day. And the cheesecake that she made only once a year. The "recipe" was actually a Jell-O box mix, but she added cream cheese, and extra butter and sugar. (My family didn't understand what people meant when they said a particular food was "too rich.")

I'd come home from college for the weekend, and after everyone had gone to bed, I sneaked into the kitchen like a cat burglar. I knew every creak in the stairs, every squeak in the hardwood floor down the hallway, the point at which the suction of the fridge would pop when you pulled the door open. I painstakingly peeled back the foil on the pan. In the middle of the night on a secret mission, foil can reach approximately 150 dB. It was just going to be a nibble. Then suddenly, an entire long thin row was missing. It was crooked, so I ate more to even it out—as if that would help camouflage that I'd eaten it in the first place.

My mother discovered it first thing in the morning and was furious and immediately blamed me. In spite of five kids, two in-laws, my father and a dog in the house, she assumed I had eaten it. I was outraged, and loudly declared my innocence. At the very least, I deserved the decency of being a *possible* suspect. At least put me in a lineup.

My mother never let it drop and it came up over and over and over again in the thirty-plus years since. She would shoe-horn it into some completely unrelated conversation. I got mad every single time. I denied it every single time. My mother was unperturbed, shrugged a shoulder, and continued on with the conversation with maybe just a little twitch of *gotcha* on her lips.

There were a lot of books before my mother started her record-keeping. I can still see the covers of *Dr. Zhivago, Gone With the Wind, Lonesome Dove, The Shipping News, The Onion Field, Bonfire of the Vanities, The Thorn Birds,* and *Fat Is a Feminist Issue.* I did not like that book even though I'd never read it. I took the long way around it wherever it might be in the house, and I never picked it up to read the back cover, like I did with all her other books. I was afraid I'd be guilty of being fat by association, if people should see me in too close proximity to the book. I'd been born pudgy, and stayed pudgy, and I didn't want anyone to know.

Then my mother read *The Women's Room.* It was the late 1970s, the height of the women's movement, and all my mother's friends had read it. Marilyn French's feminist novel tells the story of some women who married in the 1950s to the domestic bliss promised them, only for their husbands to leave them for younger women. Day after day, the hefty hardcover rested on her lap as she sat in her reading chair. My mother was pressed against the brown plaid upholstery of the colonial-style armchair, jaw set, breathing through flared nostrils as she turned the pages. She seemed mad a lot after that book.

I can practically hear her irritation about certain books.

Be Mine
Kasichke, Laura
Boring - I read 55 pages. Thriller but nothing thrilling.

Last Get Back Boogie
James Lee Burke
Read about ½-a real waste of time

South of Broad
Pat Conroy
6/10
Seemed a bit self-serving & windy - over 500 pages

Twelve Sharps + Lean Mean 13
Evanovitch, Janet
6/10
Same old, same old.

Bag of Bones
King, Stephen
6/10
*Widow writer falls for widow woman + small child with much super-
natural stuff.*
Much too long, 732 pages.

While I Was Gone
Miller, Sue
5/10
*Young woman leaves husband in the 60s to feel freedom + lives in group
house of about 6 or 7 people. One young woman is murdered. Book gets
long and preachy.*

Amnesia Nights
Skinner, Quinton
Quit after about 50 pages because characters had no redeeming qualities.

Gods Go Begging
Vea, Alfredo
Two women murdered together, one black + one Vietnamese. Read over half the book 160 pages + realized I really didn't care about any of the characters. Lots of preaching about Viet Nam War which we all know at this time was stupid.

That was also about the time my mother began meditating in the brown plaid chair. A doctor recommended transcendental meditation after she'd been diagnosed with high blood pressure. Every afternoon, she sat up straight in the chair, eyes closed, hands folded on her lap and inhaling deeply. My mother was trying to find inner peace right in the middle of the living room in the middle of the house in the middle of five kids *trying* to be quiet. *Mom's meditating!* we'd holler through the house, warning each other to shut up. She'd break her silence with a roar that seemed to come from her toes and detonate in her larynx.

"Keep it down! I-am-meditating-for-chrissakes!!"

M y mother would use "brain" like a verb. *Brain*. As a verb used with an object: to smash the skull of. *Slang*. to hit or bang (someone) on the head.

When she was especially angry at any of us kids, she'd threaten, "So help me, I'll brain you." I only understood it by context: her jaw tightly clenched, but her lips still managed to fiercely articulate the words clearly. But I, always taking things literally, thought it sounded like a beneficial thing - that a brain would be bestowed, not painfully removed or damaged.

Man Walks Into a Room
Krauss, Nichole
6/10
Lost memory (24 years) due to a brain tumor.

Haunted Ground
Hart, Erin
6/10
Ireland dig in Piet Bog - discovery of head of a red headed woman preserved from 1600.

Miracle Life of Edgar Mint
Udall, Brady
8/10
7 yr old boy (Indian Reservation) head run over by mail truck.

One day when I was in fourth grade, my mother handed me a hardcover copy of *Les Misérables*. *I think you'd like this,* she said matter-of-factly. I took her at her word - moms know stuff. It was unabridged and thick and the pages dense with small type in a translated and archaic prose. It was slow going, and I'm sure I missed many, if not all, of the finer points, but I was transfixed for weeks. This was how I learned to read - not in the way of sounding out vowels and consonants, but by being thoroughly consumed by a story and wanting to disappear into it every chance I got. My mother loved the book, and I did too. Our shared appreciation was probably because bread was pivotal to the plot. I'm sure I thought it was the protagonist.

I spent a lot of time reading in my room or on a blanket in the wooded area behind our house. There were kids that I played with in the neighborhood, but I was kind of nerdy and liked to fly solo. I didn't want the other kids to discover something else to tease me about, like the little plays I acted out, usually inspired by whatever I was reading at the time. I roamed the woods and pretended I was Caddie Woodlawn or Mrs. Mike or Trixie Belden or Harriet the Spy. I'd read everything I could get my hands on about Abraham Lincoln, so he was a character in my little scenarios. He was played by a huge, stately oak tree, and I was his wife, or the daughter he never had, or aide de camp, acting out civil war stories or personal tragedies. I always told Lincoln-Tree that he had to *carry on for the sake of the Union,* and then I embraced the tree trunk as he/it left for Springfield. I bravely waved goodbye as he receded into the distance - which was me walking backwards fluttering a kerchief in farewell.

There was everything on all the shelves in the den, my father's office. *Reader's Digest Condensed Book* compilations; all the *National Geographic*s my father had saved over the years, too beautiful to be discarded. Novels and nonfiction: Arthur Schlesinger's *A Thousand Days* seemed mysterious and sophisticated and grownup. The entire 26-plus volume *World Book Encyclopedia*, *A-Z*, taking up an entire shelf and the special yearly editions at the end of the row. My parents probably stretched to afford it, but how gorgeous the collection was, the cream faux-leather and green trim of each cover and the color photographs. I set out to read the entire thing, starting with volume *A*, but got hung up on the *horse* and *dog* entries, which became worn and greasy because I ate potato chips and ice cream during repeated perusals. I examined the *N* edition, trying to figure out if there was a connection between Napoleon and Neapolitan ice cream.

I read the backs of cereal boxes and the ingredients lists on their sides as I made my way through bowls of Cap'n Crunch. There was the local library, and the bookmobile, a motorized Oz lumbering down my very own street. I could never tell if I was excited or scared. I would be encountering a librarian - I was pretty bashful and feared possible disapproval from the librarian/coachman for some breach of protocol I didn't realize. Even though my mother was fastidious about returning library books, I was afraid of accruing fines my parents could barely afford.

Last Man Standing
David Baldacci
Ten day book that had to be returned.
I lost interest and it did not seem to be as good as his earlier.

[*?*]
Jeffrey Deaver
Returned to library and can't remember.

My mother lay in the hospital bed, dying as she had lived - propped up at an angle. My mother was taking her time shuffling off the mortal coil that long February night. She'd always been slow. With her bad knees and short legs, and becoming more unsteady as she aged, she walked slowly and deliberately. "I'm coming, I'm coming," she'd say as she toddled to keep up. She always felt like she was inconveniencing everyone. Had she been conscious she would have shooed us all away.

I thought, "Oh, Mom - and right when you were at goal weight." She would have laughed and rolled her eyes. In the last year, she'd lost almost 75 pounds. She was weak and listless and could barely walk, but she'd said with a wan resolve, "If I can just keep it off..." She was dying, but she was going to get into those size 14 pants that hung in her closet, goddammit.

Street lights shone on the snow outside and cast an amber burnish through the room. It was probably the quietest we'd ever been, the five of us kids. My father suddenly looked up, wild-eyed. "Should we pray?" His gaze bounced to each of us. We weren't exactly praying people, but we were task-oriented, and it was something we could check off a to-do list. Through the night, we fell asleep randomly in hardback chairs, our heads snapping up when our snores or someone else's woke us. We took turns on a pile of hospital blankets stacked on the floor under the fabric room divider, which we pulled over us like a dangling blanket. My mother would have been annoyed that people were making such a fuss.

S he wouldn't have wanted to be *downtrodden*, a word I've only
ever heard my mother use. The dictionary definition: tyran-
nized over; oppressed; trampled upon. I can hear the impa-
tience in her voice when I come across the word in her reviews.

We Were The Mulvaneys
Joyce Carol Oates
6/10
Story of a happy family until daughter was date raped. It was very good
but painful to read. Father who blamed daughter - family fell apart.
"Get over it", another down-trodden woman.

White Oleander
Fitch, Janet
5/10
Another down-trodden woman (Oprah book) mother in prison for
murder-daughter in many foster homes.

She Came Undone (sic)
Lamb, Wally
Can't remember except down-trodden woman.

How could my mother not remember *She's Come Undone?*

My mother had raved about it and gave me her copy. The protagonist in the book starts eating compulsively after a traumatic
event, until she's almost 260 pounds. I'd never read a book where
the main character was fat - and human and real and dimensional.
Like my mother, and her mother, my weight has been up and down
my whole life. My mother went to Weight Watchers on and off for
years, and took me to my first meeting when I was 11.

The meetings were held on Monday nights in the basement of
the American Legion. You could smell the deep fried food in the
restaurant above through the low pockmarked ceiling tiles. A lady
sitting at a table took your meeting fee and rifled through a small
box for a card with your name and handwritten notations of your
weight each week. You took that card to another lady at a mechani-
cal scale. You mounted the scale and with the eraser end of her
pencil she tapped the tab back and forth until it balanced. If you
lost weight, she'd say how much aloud. But if you gained, she wrote
down the number silently and showed it to you with her hand
cupped around the card to protect your privacy. All the cards were
given to the meeting leader.

All the women (and it was rarely men) took seats at the long
metal banquet tables for a talk by the group leader, who had at-
tained goal weight. I was the youngest in the room by 15 years or
so and I rarely said anything. The leader would give a little talk
about menu planning or coping with temptation over the holidays,
and then she'd review everyone's cards one by one. She announced
how much you lost, and people would clap. If you were one of the
folks whose number had been gravely written down, she would say
something like, "Sue, looks like you had a tough week. What happened?"

One night the topic was how to burn calories: Walking. Garden-
ing. Housework. Or sexual activity, the leader said demurely. She
couldn't remember how many calories exactly. I had just read an
article in the daily edition of the *Minneapolis Star Tribune* about
this very topic, so I piped up with the answer.

The leader laughed nervously. People tittered. "She reads," my
mother offered. "A lot."

Blonde Faith
Mosley, Walter
Started out very "gross"- did not read.

Mary Mary
Patterson, James
Started + very too "corny" for me - immediate sex scene.

Middlesex
Eugenides, Jeffrey
Story of hermaphrodite. (description short and to the point!)

lmost 50 years after Weight Watchers with my mother what I remember is this: black coffee has virtually zero calories. I studied the little booklet of calorie counts you received upon joining the program, and coffee was on a very short list of calorie-free items, like water and chicken bouillon. I didn't drink coffee as a kid, but I thought this was amazing, and thought I ought to. I was always into my older sisters' books and magazines and studied the dieting and fitness articles in their *Glamour* and *Seventeen* magazines like a scholar. Exercise tips like: take stairs two at a time to build shapely legs. Sit on the floor and "walk" with your buttocks for a firm ass. In an issue of *Seventeen* a model once offered this: "Exercise is like ice cream - a little bit every now and then doesn't do anything." I can still see the pull quote on the page, right under the photograph of the model biting her lip, and her long hair ruffling away from her shoulders. (And yet, I can't remember so many of my conversations with my mother.)

I was about 11 or 12 when one night I'd crept into the kitchen for a snack. I thought I was being so quiet: I knew how much noise the silverware drawer made, at which point in its revolution the cupboard door would squeak, and how to separate the seal on the potato chip bag. Every time I ate something, snacks or at dinner with my family, it was remarked upon. Something was always said about how much I was eating or my choices. Sneaking into the kitchen was just a way to try and eat in peace, and so I binged while I was on the lam. That night, my mother came into the kitchen in her robe and threw the lights on to find me eating chips by the light of the oven. I was dipping them in mayonnaise because that's what I thought chip dip was, what with being practically the same color and consistency. I tried to act casual and distract her. I feinted with a philosophical question: "Mom, do you ever worry about your future?"

She said, "I worry about your future."

In one of my journals from around that time, I describe a fantasy of being trapped in a grocery store overnight. I wrote: *I'd bring a few necessities, such as plates, portable oven, silverware… I'd be sick of course but I think it may be worth it.*

No wonder my mother worried. I doubt she ever read my journal, but she must have known my story because it was her story, too. In the infinite recursion of the two of us, she saw herself in me and perhaps wanted to save me from what she struggled with.

Mortal Nuts
Hautman, Pete
Taco + donut people at MN State Fair.

Fried Green Tomatoes
Flagg, Fannie
9/10
Another really enjoyable kind and gentle book by the author.

Buster's Midnight Cafe
Sandra Dallas
Butte, Montana–prize fighter and movie star

Persian Pickle Club
Sandra Dallas
9/10
A group of quilters during depression in Kansas.
Involved in a murder – very good + sweet book.

My head jerked up off the metal bed rail where I'd fallen asleep when my mother's ragged breathing stopped abruptly. She had been dying for a year and a half, but it seemed so sudden. A doctor was summoned and made the official pronouncement that my mother was dead. *I could have told you that,* my sister Liz muttered, sounding just like my mother at her testiest. Liz took the wedding ring off my mother's finger and pressed it back into my palm. We stood there, stunned. Our Irish willed out over the Midwestern, and we wailed and keened. Then we just stared. There was nothing else to be done. The instant I turned to leave the hospital room was the last time I would ever lay eyes on my mother in flesh and blood, and the memory of her began fraying immediately. Hanging on to those last images of her has been like trying to clutch water.

I can see, I can hear the precise way my mother used to describe something as *dumb*. The way she said it, it was a curt summation that sounded almost onomatopoeic. Her chin retracted slightly as the hard "D" sound came out, then her mouth went slack with the drawn out "m" at the end. At the same time, she'd give her head a little shake and her eyes narrowed a bit as the "mb" hung in the air, like an underline. And if the some of the dumb books were *really* dumb, she didn't even bother with a rating.

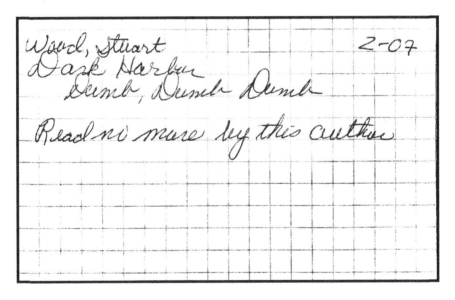

Dark Dreaming Dexter
Lindsay, Jeff
Dumb.

On The Run (?)
Johansen, Iris
Dumb dumb dumb - quit after about 30 pages

Lady Killer
Scottline, Lisa
About as dumb as possible.

Shadows
Buchanan, Edna
5/10
Dumb. Read no more by this author.

Killing Hour
Gardner, Lisa
Dumb characters. Quit before 50 pages.

Dirty Blonde
Scottline, Lisa
Dumb! But easy.

Closet
Zimmerman, R.D.
Really dumb – read about 30 pages.

My phone rang in a Target store one day. "Mom and Dad" came up on the caller ID. I hated taking calls in public, but it was almost 5 p.m. - practically my parents' bedtime - so it must have been important.

"M.J.?" It was my father, as if he were unsure who he was calling. "Your mother—"

He gulped deeply, almost a choking sound. In the middle of women's accessories, I started yelling into the phone.

"Dad! Dad! What is it? What's going on?"

I heard my mother in the background.

"Oh, for heaven's sake, Jerry, give me the phone." There were fumbling sounds of the phone being handed off.

"They found a spot on my lung," my mother said.

My four siblings and I threw a party for my parents' 50th wedding anniversary. A couple of hundred people gathered one afternoon in a beige, windowless "Event Room" at the Mermaid Supper Club, a sprawling restaurant/bar/bowling alley complex in a Twin Cities suburb. The only thing that distinguished the nondescript building from a semiconductor manufacturing plant was the enormous fiberglass mermaid on the flat roof. A kitschy landmark for decades, the mermaid held a fishing net above her head, and long fiberglass tresses - sometimes black, sometimes blonde - flowed decorously over her bare breasts. When I was a kid, driving the five miles to "the 'Maid" from our small town to a closer-ring suburb felt quite continental, but I was always embarrassed when the mermaid came into view and looked away.

My parents each took a turn at the microphone to make a toast. My father, a farm boy, was still tall and robust. My mother was short next to my father - next to almost everyone, really - and my father lowered the microphone for her. She was a city girl - that's how her in-laws viewed her, what with coming from a town of 1500. My mother waved a half-full wine glass to punctuate her philosophical musings about marriage. Her cheeks were flushed from a few sips of wine. Her father had been an alcoholic, but she could barely stand a tiny bit of anything before her tawny cheeks got red and she got overly talky and her hands moved around dramatically.

"Having five children really strengthened our marriage. We knew we had to stick together. Otherwise the kids would turn on us like a pack of wolves."

People laughed. My mother was not one to romanticize anything.

Tara Road
Maeve Binchy
0/10
I read about 125 pages & seemed to be going nowhere.
Seemed to be about 1 step above a romance novel.

Queen Fool
Gregory, Philippa
7/10
Takes place in time of Queen Mary and ½ sister Elizabeth – daughter of
Henry 8.
Turned into a bit of a romance novel.

Dying To Please
Howard, Linda
5/10
Romance novel trying to pass as a mystery. Dumb.

Every Breath You Take
McNaught, Judith
Quit after about 50 pages. A romance novel pretending to be a mystery.

Mercy
Garwood, Julie
5/10
Myst. started out good but turned into more of a romance novel.

My father accidentally asked my mother on a date. That's how my mother liked to tell it. It was the early 1950s, and my mother moved to St. Paul after high school. She got a job as a secretary at a Catholic church and shared an apartment with four other girls in an old mansion on stately Summit Avenue. There weren't a lot of options in those days, she said. Women became teachers, nurses or secretaries - but only until you got married.

My father also moved from a farm in northwestern Minnesota to the Twin Cities after high school. He had friends in that same apartment building, and when he came over for a game of poker one night, he rang the one doorbell that served the entire building. All five girls in my mother's apartment came to see who was at the door: all 6'2, 150-rawboned-pounds of crew-cutted and square black glasses of Jerry Pehl. A few days later he called their apartment. *I think he thought I was Mary Ellen,* my mother insisted. *But he was just too nice to say anything.*

My father would throw his head back and laugh his big laugh every time my mother told her version. Shaking his head vehemently and waving his hands to shoo away such a preposterous notion, he'd laugh. "No, noooooo!" He'd catch his breath: "Your mother was beautiful and easy to talk to, as if I'd known her all my life." They were both 20 when they got married less than a year later.

I believe both versions of the story. She was beautiful. She was easy to talk to - total strangers would tell her their life story. I don't think she ever said as much about the two of them, but I wonder if she thought it had to have been sheer luck that a nice looking, hard-working, straight-arrow guy would fall for a non-skinny Dorothy McNamara before she became an old maid at 21.

At the anniversary fete, I took my turn at the microphone to offer a toast and direct people to the buffet. I told my mother's version of the story. "And here we are," I said, "Fifty years, five children, 13 grandchildren later - all because of a big misunderstanding.

"Sorry we made you all come out today."

Child's Book of True Crime
Hooper, Chloe
8/10
Teacher in Australia (Tasmania) affair with married man. Interesting partly due to the history of this penal island.

Clean Cut
Monsour, Theresa
6/10
Police officer (woman) married to a doc (on + off) MN author. Serial murder by another doc.

Girl Who Married Lion
McCall Smith
(no rating)
Short stories handed down thru generations in Africa. Told to author by children, parents + grandparents.

I woke up in my parents' spare bedroom a few hours later, not knowing where I was.

Ah, yes! – my mother died a few hours ago, a million years ago.

We'd gotten home from the hospital just before daybreak, after they'd come to fetch my mother's body, and there was nothing left to be done. My sister drove my father and me back to his house, my father giving her directions to avoid road construction or snowplows. It was his habit, undeterred. I lay in bed staring at the ceiling. I assume it was the ceiling - I didn't have my contacts in - and I ran my fingers over my chin, looking for stray hairs. Had I had my wits about me to pack my contacts and tweezers when I left Austin the night before?

Upstairs, my brothers had arrived and were already at work in the kitchen with their cups of coffee. My younger brother Mike was bent over his laptop and a spreadsheet of tasks for my mother's funeral. Jim, the youngest, was in the middle of a phone call with the church's luncheon committee. It didn't matter if it was a crisis or a celebration, my family always went full-on logistical. Checking off things on a list kept us going.

I looked for my mother's tweezers in the bureau in the living room. The chest of drawers was an enormous piece of Chinoiserie she had gotten decades earlier, one of three similarly matching pieces she'd found in the want ads. The black enameled bureau functioned as a huge side table between recliners. The recliners, together with a barge-like matching sofa, were in a muted green and maroon print, atop a thick pile rug that was also green and maroon but a different print. There was a multi-headed, multi-colored table lamp in an 80s interpretation of a Tiffany lamp on a small table between two burgundy velvet Victorian-style chairs, which was next to a mammoth dish cabinet that matched the bureau. All the furniture was against the walls, as if the room had been cleared for a square dance. My mother's random and promiscuous aesthetic could be summed up by "I liked it" and/or "It was on sale."

The tweezers were always in the corner of the top drawer, tucked among books, loose photographs, old newspaper clippings, and an archaic electronic organizer that my mother used as her address book. The floor lamp behind her chair had an adjustable arm which she could position like a dentist's lamp to light her face. My mother could still maintain a conversation while she plucked her chin hairs. We didn't stand on ceremony, apparently, and the exaggerated thrust of her chin often garbled her words as she spoke.

I rooted through the drawer, but the fine tweezers were nowhere to be found. They had *always* been there. Had they been cremated with my mother? In some sort of miracle of time travel where one of us quickly drove to the house, found them, drove back to the hospital and put them with her, grave goods before the body had been taken away? Maybe my mother hid them somewhere, knowing she'd never wake up from her nap, and she'd have the last laugh because my sisters and I were always helping ourselves to her tweezers. Things were always disappearing with five kids. It hit me: she was not there to ask.

Vanishing Act
Perry, Thomas
7/10
Indian woman helps people who are in trouble disappear.
Could have been shortened without the loss of anything.

Place of Execution
McDermid, Val
9/10
Small private hamlet disappearance of 14 yr. Old girl – stepfather mo-
lester.

[Postcards]
E. Annie Proulx
Very good
Loyal Blood murders his lover by accident + disappears.

I don't recall the doorbell ringing or anyone knocking, I don't remember anyone coming or going, but food started arriving at the house. Countertops disappeared under hot dishes, jello salads, pasta salads, pies and plates of bars. Tupperware and foil-covered dishes as far as the eye could see, inching their way beyond the kitchen and onto a bench in the entryway, and the coffee table and fireplace mantel in the living room. A gorgeous Hudson Valley School landscape of carbs and sweets everywhere you looked. I was sorry my mother had to miss it.

My sisters arrived to start on the to-do list, and my father started making phone calls. He began each conversation casually, asking how the other person was. His voice got wobbly and he'd say, "I'm afraid I have some bad news about Dorothy…" Over and over again we heard the same conversation through the walls as he scrolled through my mother's little electronic address book for everyone's phone numbers. My siblings and I padded by each other aimlessly, freshening up coffees and peeling back foil and plastic lids and hollering at each other for sampling right out the container with the same fork they'd just eaten from.

Funeral Food
Taylor, Kathleen
7/10
Charming funny mystery small S.D. town.
Murder in town cafe, daughter finds the mother guilty.

Chili Queen
Sandra Dallas
9/10
Addie French madam of a brothel befriends woman on a tram. Scam artists.

Dairy Queen Days
Inman, Robert
8.5/10
Preacher + son (wife with nervous breakdown) try to find their way in small town.

My parents liked to "doctor up" food, and they used the verb to entice me to have dinner with them. *Come on over, we're going to doctor up a pizza.* It meant taking a pre-packaged item, like frozen pizza or lasagna, then adding more stuff to it. Whatever was in the fridge: leftover ham or sausage or crumbled up hamburger, or chopped up onions or peppers, or more cheese, all sprinkled on top. In our family, it was just a given to put more food on food.

My mother was more of a *preparer* of food than a cook. She made tater-tot hot dish from a church cookbook recipe, complete with ground beef, mushroom soup, canned corn, and frozen tater-tots. There were crock pot dinners she threw together in the morning that were ready when she came home from work. Her pot roast was melt-in-your-mouth, French-chef-kiss delicious. Butter was a key ingredient in the pot roast. Butter and sour cream were side dishes in our house. She made recipes found on food packages, like meatloaf with dry onion soup mix. *You know, you can use it in practically anything,* she'd counseled many times. The only recipe she ever handed down to me was instructions for hard boiled eggs. I still have to refer to the instructions she wrote out on a "From the Kitchen Of..." note card she'd found at a garage sale.

My brother assigned the obituary to me. "You're the writer in the family," Mike said, checking it off of his spreadsheet. I didn't know where to start, so I hewed to the newspaper's recommended bullet points.

Minneapolis Star Tribune suggested format for an obituary:

◊ Full name (bold print = 2 or 4 lines of space): Dorothy Therese McNamara Pehl
◊ Age: 79
◊ Date of birth: March 19, 1934
◊ Date of death: February 10, 2014
◊ City: Fridley
◊ Preceded in death by: Thomas, grandson; sisters Margaret and Katherine; parents Joseph and Bernadette.
◊ Survived by: Gerald (Jerry), husband of 59 years, and children Therese (Frank); Elizabeth (Drew); Mary Jo (Alan); Michael (Anne); and James (Cynthia); thirteen grandchildren and a great-granddaughter.
◊ Visitation information (day, time, location): 2/13, 5-7 p.m. and 2/14, 9:30-10:30 a.m. at St. Joseph's
◊ Service information (day, time, location): Mass of Christian Burial, Friday, February 14, 10:30 a.m., St. Joseph's Catholic Church
◊ Interment: cremated
◊ Memorial preferences (if any): Memorials to the local food shelf and educational foundation.

Nothing about any "courageous battle with cancer." My mother would have tightened her lips and fluttered her eyes at any such boilerplate. She wouldn't have called it *courageous* to just acquiesce to a standard protocol of chemotherapy and radiation. You want courageous? My mother went to Costco the day before she died - a Saturday.

My mother's existence - complicated, rich, layered human being existence - reduced to data points.

In her terse book reviews, she manages to summarize the most outlandish and convoluted plots. Would that I had the wherewithal to do the reading version of *Julie and Julia: My Year of Cooking Dangerously,* in which Julie Powell chronicles every one of the 524 recipes in Julia Child's *The Joy of Cooking* over the course of a year. But this is hundreds of books, I'm a slow reader, and I'm already in my mid-50s.

> Koontz, Dean,
> House of Thunder)
> 12/99
> Very dumb book about
> Russians kidnapping beautiful
> girl, keeping her drugged &
> pretending she is in USA
> twro hospital rather than
> special made uptown in
> Russia made to look USA
> 2 out of 10

Total Control
D. Baldacci
6/10
Very convoluted plot involving attorney, her husband and pilot.
Airplane sabatoged killing 200 in order to kill one person.

Hunting Down Amanda
Klavan, Andrew
8/10
Good myst + thriller about 5 yr. old bad guys are trying to kidnap
because she has some healing power.

When Wind Blows
Patterson, James
5/10
Children of illegal experiments who could fly. Not much of a thriller –
kind of dumb.

Perfect Witness
Siegel, Barry
7/10
Dunes of CA is location(?). Attorney accused of murder of postmaster.
Defended by his partner. Lots of side stories involving environmental
abuse.

Fast Forward
Mercer, Judy
6/10
Myst. Ariel suffers from amnesia. Someone trying to kill her + she can't
figure out why.

I f she had written her own obituary, my mother probably would have described herself as "average." She'd said it about herself many times with a small, offhand shrug and a wry pucker to her mouth. Her friends fussed about this assessment, and assured her she had many fine qualities. One friend told her to stand in front of the mirror and say nice things to herself every day. They didn't get it. It's so very Midwestern, such a low-key characterization of one's self, and pretty much my mother. It was not a bad thing - you could do much worse than average.

Rapture of Canaan
Reynolds, Sheri
So-so.

Resistance (?)
Shreve, Anita
2nd WW - Belgium. So-so.

Harm's Way
White, Stephen
So-so.

Plum Island
DeMille, Nelson
So-so.

Hunters Moon
Logan, Chuck
(no rating)
MN North Woods thriller - so so.

Time To Hunt
Hunter, Stephen
8/10
Sharp shooters from Viet Nam war (one Russian + one American) –
many years later are pitted against each other. Cover up of "mole" activ-
ity. Intriguing + good reading.

Once I thought she could do magic.

I was in third grade when she showed me she could type without looking at the keyboard. I have no idea how it even came up, but when she told me, I was astonished and I demanded she prove her wizardry. The old Selectric was in the den, an enormous office where my father moonlighted preparing people's income taxes. The desk was a sprawling trapezoid shape he'd designed to fit the odd-shaped room, and it was covered with inlaid red vinyl. My mother rolled a piece of blank paper into the platen and snapped the paper release lever against it. She closed her eyes and started tapping away really fast, impossibly fast. She whisked the paper out of the roller bar with its whirring-clicking sound and handed it to me. I'm sure my nine-year-old mouth was hanging open when I read a complete, coherent sentence without a single mistake: *The quick brown fox jumped over the lazy dog*. Typed out three times.

I made her do it again, and this time, I stood behind her covering her eyes with my pudgy hands. Another flawless, typo-free sentence was tapped out: *Now is the time for all good men to come to the aid of their country*. In my memory I am staring at it with my mouth agape, and maybe my mother seems a little triumphant. As if to say, *I know things. I can do things. Beyond 'mother'. I was something, I was a person, before you came along.*

Laughing Sutra
Salzman, Mark
9/10
Chinese boy + magical companion sneak into USA to find a long lost Buddhist scroll.

The Disapparation of James
Ursu, Anne
7/10
Magic trick – boy disappears into nowhere for a week.

Between food and visitors and calls, we stumbled through the first day after my mother's death *not knowing if we were on foot or horseback,* as my mother described discombobulation. Later that night, we wrapped up leftovers, and what wouldn't fit in the overflowing fridge was put in the garage to stay chilled. Hours later, I woke to sounds of crashing and thumping throughout the house. In that disoriented space between sleep and awake, I thought maybe clumsy movers had arrived to take everything away. There was a gutteral wailing from somewhere, and suddenly my father was pounding on the door.

"M.J.! Get up! I want to tell you about your mother!" he hollered.

The house was ransacked. Storage containers had been dragged from under the stairs and contents dumped on the couch or chairs. Desk and dresser drawers were pulled open and stuff had fallen out of them. The man who had followed us around turning off lights we'd left on now had the entire house lit up like an airfield. My father shoved a photo album under my nose as I pulled on my robe.

"This is when your mother moved to St. Paul and put herself through modeling school."

My mother was gorgeous, with her classic oval face and Greek nose, but height and conventional model slimness were not her long suits.

"Oh! You mean - like comportment school?" I asked, starting to get my bearings.

"That's it! Comportment school! She wanted to learn how to dress and put on makeup—she wanted to fit in when she moved to the city."

My father adjusted his enormous trifocals and turned pages, running his fingers along the images and murmuring to himself. There was the faded color photograph from the day my parents got engaged. They're standing in front of someone's house, and my mother has a yellow flower behind her ear that my father has just plucked from the bushes behind them. She is looking downward at the grass, and he is gazing at her. There's a black and white picture of her in front of her uncle's farm house. She's about high-school age, and she stands in the middle of the photograph looking straight at whoever is taking the picture. One of her aunts, a nun in a wimple and long black habit, and her mother stand in the foreground as children play around her on the grass. Everyone else seems to be in motion, as if the world is swirling around my mother. My father turned his head now and then so his nose, runny from crying, wouldn't drip on the pages.

I picture my mother vehemently vacuuming through the house. She usually had a dishcloth thrown over her shoulder, no matter what she was doing, and she had a thick, white swath of depilatory lotion on her upper lip, making her look like a stout, pissed off Sam Elliott. Sometimes there were ill-timed fights with her when she'd holler at me with that white mustache. I hated being yelled at, but it was also mesmerizing to watch the foam wiggle around on her upper lip as she took me to task for something. She always seemed mad when she vacuumed. Probably because she had to vacuum. It was never-ending with five kids.

One year everyone forgot her birthday, and she was vacuuming about it. I hid in my room, the *vroooooming* vibrating through the house. I lay on my stomach on the shag carpeting that needed to be raked weekly, and under the three cheesy, mass-produced animal portraits on the light-blue walls: a kitten, a puppy, a horse. When I wasn't watching TV, I was in my room reading and writing poetry and daydreaming. Once a week I rode my bike up to Hanson's Drugstore to buy the latest issue of Mad Magazine with my allowance and lay in supplies of candy and Cracker Jack which I hid in my room. The *vroooooming* inched closer to my closed door, and the door rattled on its hinges. Then the vacuum nudged the door, tap tap tap as she got every inch of the carpet.

The "Theme From Mahogany" came on my clock radio. I started crying as Diana Ross sang, "Do you know where you're going to... do you like the things that life is showing you..." I sobbed. *I didn't know where I was going to, and I didn't like the things life was showing me and I was already 14 years old -- and I forgot my mother's birthday!*

My mother hit the big city and attended comportment school and just like that found herself knee-deep in household appliances and five ingrate kids. Kids can really mess up their parents.

Hostage
Robert Crais
8.5
3 losers break into a home after a holdup & hold father & kids hostage.
Chief of Police Tally in this small town becomes involved with what
turns out to be the "mob". Very good page turner.

Henry Patter (sic)
Read first in a series. A very good modern day fairy tale –
good to know what kids are talking about.

Shell Seekers
Pilcher, Rosamonde
6/10
Woman goes thru 2nd WW. Father a famous painter in England,
three ingrate children.

Saving Faith
David Baldacci
FBI & CIA turf type war. Woman targeted for death and her boss who
lobby for children in 3rd world countries know too much.

Jim The Boy
Tony Earley
8/10
Simple story of a boy being raised by his widowed mother and three
bachelor uncles. Short + enjoyable.

In The Presence of The Enemy
George, Elizabeth
English – a bit slow but very good. Mystery kidnapping of 2 children.
Editor of scandal magazine.

Liz handed me a piece of paper with her handwritten notes. "This is as far as I got on the eulogy - you know how to talk in front of people." Yes - as a standup comedian. Liz is a longtime elementary-school teacher, used to dispatching orders and used to being obeyed. I'm the youngest sister, used to complying. I turned on my father's enormous computer to start writing; it was so old I swear I heard levers clanking. I stared at the blank screen. Something popped into my head.

My mother used to say, *Wake up, wake up! This is the day they give babies away!* On big and exciting days, she'd burst into our bedrooms in high spirits and throw the lights on. Maybe the first day of school, or the Minnesota State Fair, or favorite cousins coming for a visit. *Wake up, wake up! This is the day they give babies away!* I hadn't thought of it in ages. My mother's mother used to say it, and now my siblings said it to their kids. I poked around on the internet to see what I could find. It might come from an old song, dating back to the early 20th century.

"This is the day we give babies away
With a half a pound of tea
You just open the lid, and out pops the kid
With a twelve-month guarantee."

I wondered if my mother was citing that more wholesome version than a bawdier version I found.

"This is the day we give babies away;
If you know any ladies who want any babies;
Just send them 'round to me!"

M y mother was no prude, but maybe you can't take the Midwestern out of the girl.

Havana Room
Harrison, Colin
Quit on about page 60; awful people, porn language; a bore.

Stalked
Freeman, Brian
7/10
Takes place in Duluth, murder, sex club.

God Is A Bullet
Teran, Boston
0
After about 25 pages I quit – nothing but trash in a murderous cult.

By Light of Father's Smile
Walker, Alice
Quit after about 30 pages which described in detail a homosexual tryst (3 people). Decided I do not need this in my life.

I might have been in second or third grade when my mother called me into her and my father's bedroom, shut the door, and patted the king-size bed next to her. She had a pamphlet in her hand, and I scootched up on the bed next to her. "The talk" amounted to my mother reading aloud a booklet about the birds and bees provided by the Catholic church. In retrospect, it might have been the most candid conversation we ever had about sex.

It seemed to go something like this: "When a man and a woman love each other very much..." she intoned carefully, staring at the pages and avoiding eye contact. "And are married in the Holy Catholic Church... The man gives the woman a seed."

The only things I was really interested in were animals, books, television, and food. But I tried to be open-minded. I thought, *seeds? Weren't there probably some other things she wanted more than seeds? Couldn't she have used seeds from plants in the woods or something? Popcorn was basically seeds, she probably had some in the cupboard.*

"... And the seed grows inside the woman..." she continued.

This was getting preposterous. *Do women have soil inside them? There's already dirt out in the yard, wouldn't it be more efficient just to use that? In some sort of planter? The kind we saw all the time at garage sales?*

"...Then God gives the married man and woman a baby..."

I didn't want to bother my mother with all these questions, so I just nodded. I guessed this was another one of those things that everyone else was on board with, which made no sense to me.

Sex + Salmonella
Taylor, Kathleen
6/10
Tony (?) Bauer, waitress in small South Dakota town
murder of a carney person.

W̲e all babbled over each other during our meeting with the priest at our old parish to plan the funeral, the way we always had, the way that had always given my mother headaches. Father Steve was a "new" priest, in that he wasn't the same priest who had been at St. Joe's 40 years ago when our family went to Mass every Sunday. My mother went to Mass longer than any of us, but eventually stopped going too. She was angry - *disgusted,* she'd say, her chin retracting as if to underline the word as she said it - by *The Church.* But every now and then she'd sneak into a Mass at a random church. *Well, you just don't stop being Catholic.*

A few days later, my brothers, sisters, in-laws, and nieces and nephews took up three front pews, with my father anchoring the end of one. The same pews I'd sat in as a child, where I'd unconsciously imitate the priest's elaborate gesturing during parts of the Mass. My mother's eyes never left the priest, but she'd lower her arm over mine as subtly as possible to stop the miming.

In the homily, Father Steve invoked the funeral chestnut "Gone From My Sight." The poem makes the analogy that when someone dies, it's like a ship leaving a harbor. All the people they're leaving are heartbroken, waving goodbye from the shore as the dearly departed departs. *There she goes!* they cry. But—all the loved ones who've passed are excited to meet her on the other side, and they wave in welcome.

Here she comes!

"I'm sure Mom would really appreciate being compared to a ship," Therese muttered on my right, through the same set jaw my mother used to get. On Father Steve's cue, I went up to the lectern to give the eulogy, knowing my siblings will never let me hear the end of it if I bomb at my mother's funeral. My mother always got nervous at my shows, so she didn't often come. She couldn't bear the idea that I might fail in front of all these people. *You just always feel so bad for your kid if something goes wrong for them,* she said. I cleared my throat and took a breath. I'd never had to follow a priest before. This much I knew: Keep to my time, and watch for the light.

I spoke about *this is the day they give babies away.* I spoke about how my mother always said *just show up.* If there was something you were dreading, if you were scared, if you were at a loss about what to do - just show up. That's half the battle, she said with a little nod of certainty. You'll figure it out when you get there. One step at a time. She'd shown up for a husband and five kids and figured it out along the way. I didn't choke up when I talked about her, and the laughs came at the right places. My peripatetic comedy career had served me adequately.

Way back when, when my mother ever dying was apocryphal, we'd pretend-plan our funerals, like planning the perfect wedding or how we'd spend lottery winnings. She always said she wanted a Dixieland band at her funeral. And thus, the solemn Rite of Commendation gave way to a headache-inducing blaring brass band playing "When The Saints Go Marching In" through the church hallways, leading the congregation to the social hall for lunch.

We family were first in line at the buffet and I could practically hear my mother's exasperation as I made my way through the spread: buttered white buns with prepackaged ham slices, soupy pasta salad, and wan vegetable platters.

Carrot sticks? This is a funeral, not a Weight Watchers meeting. I'm so disgusted.

7th Heaven
Patterson, James
7/10
Womens Murder Club mystery. Arson fires by two young men.

Undomestic Goddess
Kinsella, Sophie
7/10
Cute.

Can't Wait To Get To Heaven
Flagg, Fannie
9/10
Another really enjoyable kind and gentle book by the author.

Lovely Bones
Sebold, Alice
9/10
Story of 14 year old's view from heaven following her rape + murder.
View of her family + friends trying to cope.

Pigs In Heaven
Kingsolver, Barbara
Taylor leaves home + adoption of turtle. Great - turtle abandoned +
adopted by white woman - Cherokee nation wants her back.

Once I asked my mother, "If you could ask God anything, what would you ask him?" She didn't hesitate, as if she'd given it a lot of thought.

"I'd want to know why I didn't get skinny legs. And… I'd probably ask why he put everything so close together on women. For pete's sake - the vagina, the uterus, the bladder, anus… It's a mess down there."

Envy
Susan Brown
7/10
OK. Suggested by Jan Harris. Easy reading.

My mother took other women's bodies personally. Certain legs annoyed her - long legs that went straight down from hip to ankle, uncomplicated by superfluously fleshy thighs like hers. If I was wearing shorts or a swimsuit, she'd appraise mine. My legs were big but at least, my mother observed, I didn't have the *drip*. The "drip" was what she called flesh from her thighs that just stopped at her knees and pooled there, leaving completely normal calves. She'd say the word with a hand motion like something spilling out of her palm, and do kind of a "blurp" with her mouth to underscore the word. *The injustice,* she'd say, with narrowed eyes as she'd watch a woman effortlessly striding by, thighs that didn't seem to rub together. *You have nice ankles,* my mother once remarked. I grit my teeth. *I will certainly put that in my personals ad and my online dating profile,* I said.

Dive From Clausen's Pier
Packer, Ann
7/10
Diving accident causes Mike to become a parapalegic.
Fiance can't take + takes off for NY.
I got tired of all the whining + melodramatics but was taken in by it.

I t was one of my first road trips of my standup comedy career, and I was the opening act at the Westward Ho in Grand Forks, North Dakota. The first night of the weekend gig, I tripped and fell coming off the stage after my set, and I sprained my leg something terrible. I was either scared to go to a doctor, or I didn't have insurance, but probably mostly, I didn't want to bother anyone with my silly clumsiness. Months later I was still hobbling around, and my mother asked how my leg was. I told her that it was still painful and seemed to be taking a long time to improve.

"Well," she said crisply, "some people don't have legs."

It was her way of saying *stop feeling sorry for yourself.* Be grateful that at least you have appendages to be in pain. As if to say, *Think of all the people who would give anything to have a bum leg.* It became a catch phrase among my siblings, a shorthand to stop ourselves from dwelling on anything or being sentimental about anything. We try to make each other laugh instead.

Rifling through all the little reviews, I came across another word that I'd only ever heard my mother use: *hokey*. I'd only understood it by its context and the way her mouth curled downward with a soupçon of derision. But now, I actually looked it up in the dictionary: *Mawkishly sentimental or contrived; corny.*

Midnight Before Christmas
William Bernhardt
6/10
Easy reading–hokey story about ex-cop whose wife
is setting him up to murder him and collect 3 million.

Plain Truth
Picoult, Jodi
6/10
Amish girl hides her pregnancy–baby dies + she accused of murder.
Easy reading but hokey.

Sweetwater Creek
Siddon, Anne Rivers
Got long and hokey.

Orchid Beach
Woods, Stuart
5/10
Installation of drug cartel in Fla (big as a military installation).
Author recommended by Ron Stephens but I thought a bit hokey.

Tailspin
Catherine Coulter
Hokey. Read to page 64. Read no more by this author.

My mother had a heart attack in her early 60s, a minor one considering she'd had the wherewithal to ask the EMTs if they could stop at Costco on the way to the hospital. It was the big grand opening of a new store, and free memberships were being offered for only that day. She brushed it off, saying it was a joke. I highly doubt it.

She followed doctors' orders to the letter in her recovery and seemed to be doing just fine. But after one routine follow-up visit, she got a message on the answering machine the night before Thanksgiving. A nurse with a chipper Minnesota accent said, *Hi, Dorothy – the latest tests don't look so good, but you can discuss it with the doctor at your appointment next week.* The nurse signed off with a breezy, "Now don't let this information ruin your holiday weekend!"

I was home to spend the night when she listened to the message, and I was sitting in the recliners with her, angled toward the picture window where my parents loved to watch the neighborhood. It had been a good 20 years since the Cheesecake Incident, and I don't remember if it even came up or if there was even cheesecake in the fridge. She took off her reading glasses and set her book on her lap. Out of nowhere, she said, "I'm just not ready to say goodbye to the grandchildren." We hadn't been talking about anything in particular, and suddenly she was trying not to cry.

I froze. In the same moment, she might just as easily slip her reading glasses back on her nose and say something like, *I guess it'll all work out. Or it won't.* And shrug a shoulder and open the book again. My mother had given birth to five children and raised them; she'd had a hysterectomy and knee replacement surgery. A heart attack. And head colds: she got colds often and always said through her sniffles: "Colds just seem to hit me harder than anyone else." But she always survived. She led us to believe she was invincible.

Interpreter of Maladies
Lahiri, Jumpha
9/10
Short stories.

Guardian of Lies
Martini, Steve
10 day book. Got started. Got sick. Returned. Lost interest.

A Civil Action
Harr, Jonathan
8/10
Case history of a courtroom showdown. 8 families + cluster cases of leukemia + other cancers probably due to wells (city) contaminated by two large companies. Got technical but very good. Woburn, Mass is the city.

Poisonwood Bible
Kingsolver, Barbara
9.5/10
Baptist missionary takes family to Africa - wife + 4 daughters. He is very narrow and misguided. One daughter dies of snakebite.

Unnatural Exposure
Patricia Cornwall
4/10
Dr. Kay Sarpetti series, she is an ME… this was on boring side.
Smallpox outbreak + dismembered bodies.

Sometimes I asked my mother: *If you had to do it all over again, would you have had children?* She always tilted her head to one side and gave pretty much the same answer, but it started to sound different the older I got and the more life I lived. My mother had her first child, my oldest sister Therese, ten months after she and my father got married. Liz, number two, was born 14 months later. Four years later, there was me, and then my two brothers, Mike and Jim, four and seven years after me.

"Oh… there are lots of things I probably would have done differently. We didn't really think about it back then. We just… did it."

After a pause, she added: "Maybe not so many."

I asked her what she thought about my not having children.

"I'm not surprised. You never played with dolls - you never played 'house' like other little girls."

Still, I was very much in demand as a babysitter when I was a teenager. It really wasn't so much about child care as it was watching old movies on network television and raiding the refrigerator. At 50 cents an hour plus tip, I could pocket upwards of $3 for a night of eating and television. The kids were kind of beside the point.

One night I came home in tears from a babysitting job. I'd let the kids stay up later than they were supposed to, and they weren't in bed when the parents got home. They took me to task, and I was mortified. I walked the two blocks home, and I collapsed on the floor next to my mother reading in her chair. I was disgraced! I was sure my career was over. *I'll never babysit in this town again,* I sobbed into her leg. My parents invariably demanded what us kids had done to warrant getting into trouble. But this time, my mother just stroked my hair as I cried. *You take things too seriously, Mairzy Doats.*

The Rainbow
Flagg, Fannie
8/10
Dorothy in the 1940s homemaker broadcast radio show from her home in MO. Story of many lives in this small town including race for the Gov. seat by a shy woman.

Last Juror
Grisham, John
7/10
Different from others – small town newspaper editor in South.

Where You Once Belonged
Haruf, Kent
9/10
Small town story of two boys growing up –
one a jerk the other inherits a newspaper.

The monthly mortgage on my parents' first house was $97. It was 900 square feet of the post-war housing boom in Circle Pines, Minnesota, about half an hour north of St. Paul. The small town had been founded as a planned cooperative community, a type of city model started in the 1940s. Homeowners owned shares in an association which managed the city's own utilities. The symbol for a city cooperative was two pine trees within a circle, hence *Circle Pines*. The local weekly broadsheet was *The Circulating Pines*.

My father worked full-time and often moonlighted too, while my mother stayed home with kids. They were stretched thin. There's a photo from my first birthday where I'm in a high chair, digging into a piece of cake, and I've got a pie tin tied to my head with ribbon as celebratory headgear. My parents had to make do at Halloween too. We always went as hobos. Which meant my mother could take one of my father's worn-out shirts or suit jackets, make a bindle with a stick and bandana, and smudge our faces with dirt to capture the realism of us kids having hopped a rail and not having bathed for a long time.

And they had one car, which my father took each day to his job in the city. I was agog at how trapped my mother must have felt: three little kids and two more to come, in a small town or suburb, and no public transportation and nothing in walking distance. Again with the one shoulder shrug. "That's just what you did in those days - got married, had kids, the wife stayed at home with them, the husband worked."

My mother didn't even have a license, and she was terrified to learn. But she struck a bargain with their neighbor Janet. Janet would teach her to drive, and my mother would drive another licenseless neighbor and her two daughters to Mass on Sundays. Which is how eight of us crammed into a sedan with no seatbelts and three smokers, all the windows rolled up, for the drive to St. Joe's every Sunday.

In the early 1960s, my father was elected mayor. He was 26, and the city's youngest mayor to that point. One of his major accomplishments, he's proud to tell you, was instituting bulk trash pickups, all that stuff that's too large to be collected by the regular garbage collection, like mattresses and old toilets. And thus, my mother became a politician's wife. I teased her that she should have given a tour of the Crackerbox House for local television, just like Jackie Kennedy. It was more like this: people would come up to her at the grocery store or church and complain about what my father was or wasn't doing as mayor.

Once a woman called the house to gripe, and she got my mother. The woman imperiously identified herself. "This is Mrs. Dr. Steve Bergstrom!" My mother responded, "Well, this is Mrs. Mayor Jerry Pehl, and you can take it up with the Mayor himself!"

I got a vicarious thrill whenever I heard this story. My sassy mother, she with her "averageness" and only in her mid-twenties with a self-possession that I envied.

Indian Lawyer
Welch, James
7/10
Makes good in Helena, Montana after very dirt poor beginning.
Politics.

Cinnamon Gardens
Selvedurai, Shyan
British ruled Ceylon (Sri Lanka); about politics and two unhappy
people. Could not get into it. Read about 70 pages.

The Brethren
Grisham, John
8/10
3 convicts in a federal prison. - scam wealthy gay men,
including a powerful presidential candidate backed by CIA.

Turtle Catcher
Helget, Nicole
7.5/10
World War I - New Germany, MN. Got a bit "overkill" toward the end.

There were two "seasons" in our family. January to April was "tax season," a shorthand that we would barely see my father for four months as he put in long hours at his accounting office, and usually in addition to his regular job.

Summer was "garage sale season." This was when my mother would pore over the newspaper ads and seasonal listings under the heading "Garage Sale." The folded paper on her lap, my mother drove the station wagon full of us kids, sans seatbelts, cruising neighborhoods and looking for handmade signs weaving us through Circle Pines, and sometimes, excitingly, neighboring suburbs.

My mother's job was to drive slowly past the sales. It was our job to eyeball the sale from the back seat and report whether it was worth stopping for. It was nerve-racking, and I got nervous every time I had to make the call. Sometimes as the car crawled by, she'd glance at a driveway full of used wares and sniff, "That's not a garage sale, that's a junk sale." And it was eyes back on the road and foot on the gas pedal.

Prayers for Sale
Sandra Dallas
8/10
Nice book-series of short stories pulled together.

Grand Opening
John Hassler
8/10
Family moves from Minneapolis to small town
Plum to run a grocery store.

Shop Girl
Martin, Steve
6.5/10
Only 130 pages, started out better + slowly got kind of old.

Once a week my father would pick me up after school and we'd drive to the liquor store my parents owned. Rose's Liquors was in the heart of Minneapolis, and I'd work there on Wednesdays with my father from after school to closing. I was still in junior high and wasn't old enough to run the register, but I could stock the cooler and shelves and hang out by the registers. That's where the funny and cute male clerks were and where it was easy to pocket Slim Jims and the little packages of peanuts.

My mother was working there one afternoon when the crew was held up by men with guns and wearing hoods over their heads. They locked one of the clerks in the cooler and, holding a gun to her head, they made my mother lay on the floor behind the cash register. She didn't talk about it much, but when she did, she always noted that the gun had a silencer on it. She always said, "They knew what they were doing."

I want to say she was never the same after that, but how would a naive simpleton of a 15-year-old even know what that was? My mother was mysterious to me in normal circumstances. She seemed to cry a lot after that, randomly and seemingly without provocation. But we had no sense of depression or trauma back then, and I don't know if she ever talked to anyone about it - my father, a therapist, her sisters, or my older, more mature sisters. In that time, in our Midwestern culture, you just soldiered through it. You just did not want to be *downtrodden*.

Pursuit
Perry, Thomas
8/10
Story of a death match fought between a professional killer + hired gun
(illegal) by relatives of innocent victims. Kept my interest.

And Now You Can
Vida, Vandela (??)
5/10
N.Y. girl threatened by man with gun - very tiresome, self-pity.

Peace Like a River
Leif Enger
9/10
Young man shoots + kills two intruders.
Some say hero, some say killer-he escapes + what it does to family -
father alone raising 3.

Tricky Business
Dave Barry
7/10
Second mystery written by D.B. Casino ship drug runners.
Lots of shooting and some human (??) but not Carl Hiaasen.

No Second Chance
Harlan Coben
9/10
Doc and wife shot & 6-month old daughter kidnapped.

My parents sold the liquor store soon afterwards. They were always entrepreneurs, and my mother bought a card and gift shop in downtown Minneapolis. The shop had floor-to-ceiling windows along the busy hallways in the skyway system of a high rise office building, and it was people-watching heaven for my mother. From then on, we got greeting cards for almost every occasion: birthdays, Christmas, Thanksgiving, Halloween, Easter. My mother didn't sign them: *That way, you can reuse them!* my mother pointed out, proud of her practicality.

I worked part-time at the shop when I was in college. I'd always loved paper products and office supplies: stationery, notebooks, pens, envelopes, folders - and greeting cards. Perfectly cut rectangular paper of a certain heft, prettily illustrated with manufactured sentiments, ideal for someone who was always tongue-tied. I'd written some for my high-school paper, and I always kept a journal, but how could I even begin to dream about being a *real writer* like the authors of such poetry? I signed every card I gave to my parents *Mary Jo Pehl*, every anniversary, birthday, and Mother's and Father's Day cards. I wasn't sure how many Mary Jos they knew.

A grimey little transistor radio whose antenna always needed fiddling played while I waited on customers, dusted all the tchotchkes, and straightened out the disarray of greeting cards that had been savaged by people urgently needing to find a last-minute anniversary card. I sang along with a Top 40 station and fantasized about the day my real life would start, the day my ship would come in, and I'd have an important job - with benefits - in which

I was competent and admired and would be the one striding to
and fro importantly on the other side of the window. "Teach Your
Children" came on the radio. I worshipped Crosby, Stills, Nash,
and Young, and I was profoundly moved by the song. I grabbed a
discarded envelope from the trash and jotted down the lyrics.

You who are on the road
Must have a code
That you can live by
And so become yourself
Because the past is just a good-bye.

Teach your children well,
Their father's hell
Did slowly go by,
And feed them on your dreams
The one they pick's, the one you'll know by.

Don't you ever ask them "Why?"
If they told you, you will cry,
So, just look at them and sigh
And know they love you.

The next day my mother found the envelope in the trash, and
called her friend Carole. The way she told it, she was so excited to
tell Carole: "I think Mary Jo might be really talented - listen to this
poem she wrote!" My mother told me this story many years later,
and I laughed. As she remembered it, Carole seemed to hesitate,
and said it was a nice poem, but that it sounded really familiar.

No wonder my mother was skeptical about my creative endeavors.

I t felt a little shady going through my mother's closets after she died. We'd always been strictly forbidden to go in her "garage sale closets," where her bargains were stockpiled under lock and key. There were potential birthday and Christmas gifts, like crockpots and irons, utensils, clothes, pillows. There were plastic food-storage containers and panini irons and tiny, half-used sewing kits, all sorts of household items for when a grandchild launched out on their own. There were backpacks and school supplies that she accumulated over the months and then donated to the local elementary school at the start of the school year. Trash bags of fabric for some women she knew who sewed clothes for Haitian orphans. Another trash bag full of plus-size blouses for one of her cousins because *she never buys herself anything nice and it's nice to have something nice.*

My mother liked stuff. I hated stuff. Mostly I'd always been too broke to acquire much, and all my low-paying entry-level jobs went toward student loans and rent on efficiency apartments. But I got used to living austerely, and I embraced it. It felt like freedom, to be unencumbered, like I could join the Peace Corps at a moment's notice if I wanted. But every year my mother would ask what I wanted for Christmas or my birthday. Every year I would name a book or an album or a movie (when VHS came along), treasures I wouldn't have been able to afford. I never got anything on my list. My answer probably never coincided with what was in her garage sale closet at the time.

Kitchen House
Grissom, Kathleen
7/10
Good review but just above a romance novel +
below Gone With The Wind.

Except the year my mother gave me a brand new, hardcover edition of *Gone With The Wind* for Christmas. A book, an actual book. Not just a book, a brand new book. The Margaret Mitchell Anniversary Edition in its own special box. My mother had read it when she was a girl, when it was not as problematic as it is now, and back when she could remember everything and had no need of a card catalog. Over and over again she'd say with a sigh, "One of my all-time favorites."

Some time in my twenties, she took me to see the anniversary re-release of the film at an arthouse theater. I did not have a lot of time for my mother at that time. I was off pursuing my glamorous independence, living in a tiny no-bedroom apartment in a not-great part of Minneapolis and struggling to pay off student loans while working my clerical job at K-Tel International, thinking I was in the music industry. I managed, however, to make time and grace her with my presence one afternoon. My mother drove us to the theater, her line of vision barely clearing the top of the steering wheel. She said something offhand about *how sexy Clark Gable was.* A playful swooning look crossed her face and her shoulders dropped in a sort of helplessness with her hands still on the wheel. It never occurred to me that my mother took any notice whatsoever of the opposite sex. I mean, was she even allowed to, a married woman with five children?

She'd mention to my sisters and me that she found men in uniform a turn-on. "Yes, even the postman!" she declared, tilting her chin defiantly, even though no one had questioned the parameters of "uniform."

I was a late bloomer and wasn't sure what "sexy" meant. Did it have anything to do with men donating their seeds to women, which seemed to happen a lot based on all the people in the world? My mother and I took our seats, each with our own tub of popcorn as we were not a food-sharing people, lest you pull back a bloody stump. Clark Gable came on screen. My hand stopped in mid-air bringing popcorn to my mouth, and my walnut brain went "Ohhh-hhhh." It dawned on me that my mother had probably had sex. My mother knew stuff.

One day I got home from junior high and poked my head into the TV room, where my mother was watching television. She hardly ever watched television during the day, and I usually went downstairs immediately to claim the kids' television before anyone else got home so I could watch *Match Game*. *The Mike Douglas Show* was on, or maybe it was Merv Griffin, and boyishly charming entertainer John Davidson was singing. He wailed the song into the microphone he held above his head dramatically. Studio lights sparkled behind him, and sometimes he looked right into the camera, giving viewers a chance to enjoy his dimples and bounteous head of hair.

My mother was silent, until she said, "He's too cute to be trusted."

I nodded my head in solidarity, having no idea what she was talking about. It sounded mysterious and stern and kind of enticing. There was so much I didn't know and she did.

Young, Brave + Handsome
Leif Enger
8/10
MN author, man has adventure when leaving his family to accompany
an old man to Mexico. 6 weeks turned into more like 6 months.

Open House
Elizabeth Berg
7/10
Man leaves wife and she gets roomers to help pay mortgage.

Watchman
Robert Crais
8/10
Kidnap of young woman.

Alice's Tulips
Sandra Dallas
8/10
New bride of Union army man –
lives on farm with his mother during Civil War.

They're all savages," my mother said once. She was referring to *men*.

It was just so *factual* when it came out of her mouth. We might have been talking about the driving trips she and my father would take with all us little kids. She told about breast-feeding one baby or another in the passenger seat, and truck drivers rolling alongside the car. They'd look down from their cabs and stare as long as they could. Sometimes they'd pull the air horns. I wonder what she had learned from her mother. I wonder what she had learned from her own life.

"It takes women to civilize them."

Savage Run
Box, C.J.
7/10
Game warden (Joe Pickett) ranchers fighting environmental people.

Falling Man
Don DeLillo
Read about ½ and still did not get it!

Up River
DeMille, Nelson
Read about ½ of a very long, going nowhere book.
Man returns to Viet Nam for CIA. Boring.

Beyond Recall
Godard, Robert
7/10
English - man convicted of murder he didn't commit.
Story of his son + best friend. Gets pretty convoluted.

The Road
McCarthy, Cormac
9/10
Really good-father+son travel cross country 20 years after nuclear war.

Lincoln Lawyer
M. Connelly
7/10
Defense attorney-works out of back of his Lincoln car. Sleezy clients.

Until They Bring the Street Car Back
West, Stanley Gordon
8/10
Demise of streetcars in St. Paul by a local author
who went to Central High School.

Roadside Crosses
Jeffrey Deaver
Quit after about 50 pages.

Driving trips were the only kind of vacations my parents could afford when we were kids. We'd drive cross-country, visiting assorted aunts and uncles and cousins in Florida or Texas or California. We were all loaded into the car in our pajamas long before daylight, and we drove all day and ate sandwiches along the way. In the late afternoon, we would stop at a motel for the night. I was an infant for one of those trips, and my mother liked to tell how she'd use a motel dresser drawer for a crib. (I can only assume the drawer was left open.)

In the early 70s, my father modified an enormous, tan Chevy van for a trip to the brand new Disney World. He built a sleeping platform over the cargo area in the back, where my brothers and I could lay. My sisters each had one of the bench seats, and if we wanted to be upright, they had to grant permission to sit by them.

Every morning, we'd pile into the van and my father would climb in the driver's seat, put his coffee cup in the console, and say, "Wake me when we get there." It made me nervous every time. I *thought* he might be joking, but I was never quite sure. My mother rode shotgun. There was a large console between the front seats, and her arm could barely reach to rest her hand on the back of the driver's seat. We kids usually slept until we stopped for breakfast, but one morning I was barely awake when the Charlie Rich song "Behind Closed Doors" came on the radio. The transmission was quiet and crackly on that long stretch of highway, and my mother clicked off the radio. *This song is too dirty for the kids to hear,* she whispered.

She had a wooden yardstick tucked beside her seat. If we started fighting or getting wild, my mother would start whipping the yardstick behind. Perhaps it was something she learned from the nuns at Catholic school. She brandished the yardstick like a lion tamer, never looking behind her to see who might be on the receiving end. We all straightened up to save ourselves and each other. We didn't think anything of it at the time. When I was a grownup, I asked her about it. She sighed. "Survival. Probably just trying to survive."

Survive. Here she was, not even 40 and with five kids, the oldest 17 and the youngest about five. Two broke, harried parents trying to give their kids the trip of a lifetime. Maybe a yardstick seemed like a worthwhile and necessary investment.

Cloudsplitter
Russell Banks
6/10
John Brown and Harpers Ferry as told by his one surviving son –
gets very long and preachy – too much detail on battles.

Dead Survivors
Erickson, K.J.
6/10
OK story – MPLS based-murder involving the Confederate flag
that was captured by MN after huge number of (???) in an early Civil
War battle.

Flamboya Tree
Clara Olink Kelly
8/10
Dutch family in concentration camp in Java. Island taken by Japanese.
Mother keeps herself + three children alive although starving + diseased
for 4 years until they are liberated + sent back to Holland.

I was on my soapbox. My mother sighed her particular sigh of exasperation, her eyes fluttering with her special eye roll.

"Oh, M.J.... I don't know... some things are just... for fun!"

This time it was about the television show *Survivor*. My parents never missed it, and every Wednesday they ate dinner off trays on their laps with their eyes glued to the television. I'd never even seen it, but it just made me mad on principle. A group of contestants fend for themselves on a remote island, making their own food and shelter and subsisting on a bare minimum of food and clothing, especially the young female contestant. They compete in grueling competitions to try to keep themselves from being voted off the island, all for a million-dollar prize. My parents were always a little self-satisfied that they'd seen the very first episode, being early adopters and all, and they were a little bit, maybe, mostly, responsible for it being a big hit. They had no time for the hoi polloi who came to it late, like the third episode or so.

"Mom," I said sternly. "The show trivializes and commodifies for entertainment what billions of people have to actually do every single day: *survive!*" I, the woman who watched television for a living, thought my parents watched too much TV.

"Oh, MJ..." She shrugged her little one-shoulder shrug. "Sometimes I just... *enjoy* things. Sometimes I don't want to have to think about it."

The family road trips were also where I learned the "The Quiet Game."

My mother would shout over us that *whoever can be silent the longest wins!* She tried to get us to play on road trips, runs to the grocery store, or any given day in our household. "Time for the quiet game now," she would holler over us when it all got to be too much. I thought it was a bona fide game, like a board version existed somewhere with a small rule booklet tucked inside, and we just couldn't afford it. We were five voluble kids. It's not like we actually interrupted each other - we were all just talking at the same time. All this amidst radios playing, televisions blasting, friends running through the house, and whatever dog at the time barking. Not to mention each of us secretly considered ourselves an only child.

"Pleeeeeeeeeeeese." She held her hands parallel to each other and made little chopping motions as exclamation points to what she was saying. "Can't you at least talk annnnny softer?"

Long after we all left home, and it was just my parents in a big house, my mother discovered the Trans-Siberian Orchestra. Around the holidays, she'd crank their Christmas album at full blast and yell over it. "Isn't this great?" she shouted at me. She would grin with relish and her hands made little conductor movements along with the music. Was the house too quiet now? Or was she getting even? I had to ask her to turn it down. *Good god, Mom! Does it have to be that loud?*

Hour Game
David Baldacci
8/10
Serial copycat murders after different serial killers

Silent Witness
Patterson, Richard North
6/10
Attorney Tony Lloyd goes back to childhood home to defend old classmate.

Silent Snow
Thayer, Steve
7/10
Takes place in area of Selby Dale (St. Paul).
Kidnapping following details of the Lindberg kidnapping.

Monkeewrench(?)
Tracy, P.J.
8/10
Good plot about computer game + group that puts it together.

Dead Silence
Handburg, Ron
7/10
Kidnap of 3 boys, brothers - 15 years prior thought to have drowned in
Mississippi - takes place in TC.

Open Season
Box, C.J.
8/10
Game warden in Wyom. Myst about endangered species.
Easy read & entertaining.

The Woods
Harlan Coben
8.5
Summer camp murders. Good plot.

Sleepy Head
Billingham, Mark
10/04
7/10
English writer; murderer tried to keep his young female victims alive but completely paralyzed.

First Counsel
Meltzer, Brad
6/10
Young attorney working in White House gets involved with First Daughter, blackmail, and murder.

Tell No One
Harlan Coben
7/10
Good page turner mystery.
Wife killed (turned out to be kidnapped) husband dr. in Harlem.

Alone
Gardner, Lisa
6.5/10
Kidnap story of woman in 30 age range –
held 28 days underground when she was 12. A stretch.

Easy Prey
Sanford, John
Read about half of the book + could not get interested in characters. Lucas Davenport is the detective-murdered girl is a model + druggie - I'm
not nuts about Sanford's books.

Connelly, Michael   10 - 99
Blood Work

Heart transplant patient former
FBI realizes that someone is
killing certain blood types to
access vital organs
7 out of 10

B y the time I was 12 I had worry lines on my forehead, and the tales my mother brought home from her new job fanned my already anxious nature. She'd started working as an admitting clerk in the emergency room of a nearby hospital. *I'm sure we needed the money,* she said. *I knew I needed to get out of the house.* She'd get home from a shift and review who'd come to the emergency room that day. I became convinced that the most mundane, banal activity could instantly go horribly haywire. You're going about your day, tra la la, and just like that you're at the emergency room bleeding all over the place or fishing a dismembered limb out of your purse while my mother helped you fill out forms. Getting yourself a glass of tap water? Disaster. Folding laundry? Catastrophe. Sitting in your own home minding your own business? Tragedy just waiting to happen.

There was an incident that my mother brandished every summer as a cautionary tale. A guy came to the emergency after having smuggled fireworks from Wisconsin, where they were legal, to Minnesota, where they were banned at the time. The way my mother told it, he and his buddies hid the fireworks under the drivers' seat of their pickup truck, and the driver dropped a match or cigarette which then set off the fireworks. It sounds improbable as I write it, but my mother loathed fireworks. My younger brother Jim and his friends had recently been caught with contraband fireworks, and my mother hollered gory details at him. "And," my mother hissed at him, "it blew his fucking balls off!" That she said the f-word *and* referenced genitals showed she was beyond furious.

Unnatural Exposure
Patricia Cornwell
4/10
Dr. *Kay Sarpetti series, she is an ME… this was on boring side.*
Smallpox outbreak + dismembered bodies.

It started with Joseph Wambaugh's *The Onion Field*. It was agony for her to read, but she could not put it down. More books started stacking up by her bed and chair. I can't remember specific titles, but I can see the books in my head. They were the smaller, mass-market paperback size, the kind you used to find at airports. The titles were big and red, with droplets of blood dripping off some of the letters and superimposed over lurid photographs cropped in fragmented shapes, like shards of glass, just abstract enough to simply suggest their goriness.

I'd also read *The Onion Field*, at her recommendation, but I couldn't bear it. The real-life stories were too much for me. But she was desperate to talk about them, like she just couldn't help herself from disgorging the graphic details. Once she followed me from room to room trying to blurt out the gruesome particulars of one book. I kept hollering at her to stop, even if to just drown her out.

We kind of started laughing at how silly the escalation had become, but we were still yelling. I finally shut myself in the bathroom. "Stop it! Stop it!" On the other side of the door, my mother got the last word in, as usual. "And then he made her drink Drano!"

Sweater Letter
Dave Distel
9/10
Case history of murder of woman by husband who claimed it was
hunting accident.

Decidedly Game
Catherine Crier
8/10
Nonfiction – untold story of Scott Peterson investigation.

Bitter Harvest–Case History
Rule, Ann
6.5/10
Dr. Debora Green in Kansas City, MO – fire setter + kills 2 of her 3 children in an attempt to punish husband who is seeking a divorce. Also poisons him with castor beans.

There were always diets in our house for my mother and me. Diet clubs, diet programs. Regimens of five hundred calories a day, so my mother could fit into a certain dress in the months leading to each of my sister's weddings. Days of cabbage soup, and meals of sliced tomatoes (sprinkled with sugar) and cottage cheese and results obsessively monitored. My mother would fold her hands together to feel her fingers getting skinnier. "I can feel it in my hands!" she'd say gleefully.

And every time: *This time - I'm going to keep it off.*

I didn't really get that there was something wrong with me until I was about six or seven. I was tall for my age, and soft and round. Not gangly like my sisters, not just "regular" like my brothers. When I was about seven, I was at my best friend Barbie's house, and her mother sat at the dinette having coffee with a friend. The stranger scanned me up and down, and remarked to Barbie's mother, "Well, that's a big one."

Then there were diets for me too. Weight Watchers when I was in grade school. Diets that were featured in my sisters' *Glamour* and *Seventeen* magazines. In college, it was my turn for the commercial weight-loss program my mother had tried. Five hundred calories a day, and you reported to the "clinic" for a weigh-in and a motivational counseling session by a woman in a white lab coat. At that time, it wasn't common knowledge how dangerous it was. It was just very necessary that you not be fat. I should have realized it was a problem when I was doing laundry one day, and my mouth started watering as I poured the rich, viscous blue detergent into the machine. I had my own self-imposed programs: a couple of months with one or two granola bars a day and drinking Tab all day long. All the sugar and caffeine on an empty stomach made me feel like I was going insane. In my twenties and thirties, I did a couple of the pre-packaged, apportioned food programs. I always lost weight, and I always gained it back - and then some.

I lived life in my head, and I had no idea what my body was getting up to anywhere else. It was like a moat at my collarbone where I kept a safe distance from all *that*. Then I just stopped weighing myself.

Eyes of A Child
Patterson, Richard North
5/10
Murder of "rotten" father by mother-in-law.
Got very long + self serving to make it a "fat book."

Playing for Pizza
Grisham, John
7/10
Washed up football NFL player gets hired by Italian team.
Not his usual.

The Light of Evening
O'Brien, Edna
Could not get into it. Seemed very heavy.

I'd tell people about my mother's diagnosis and the reaction often was: "Did she smoke?" Not "I'm so sorry!" or "That's terrible" or "How is she?" As if her lung cancer had to be justified. She'd quit smoking in the 1970s but so what? What did it matter at this point? I stopped bringing it up except when it was necessary.

I was working a part-time day job as an administrative assistant for a medical recruiter while I was touring with a comedy group on weekends. The woman worked out of her home, and a couple of times a week I'd drive to her enormous tract home in an Austin suburb, the kind of house where lots of exterior angles and lots of odd "bonus rooms" passed for design. Pinching my lips together so I wouldn't cry and be unprofessional, I told her that I needed to go back to Minnesota for a while because my mother had lung cancer. She turned to reach up for a coffee mug in her kitchen cabinet and said offhandedly, "Well, the good thing about cancer is that it gives you time to say goodbye." Whoa. Wait a minute. No one had said anything about *dying.* I was going to Minnesota to keep my mother *alive.*

Say Goodbye
Gardner, Lisa
Kept my interest-easy reading mystery.

Say Goodbye
Mary Higgins Clark
5/10

The woman fired me a few months later.

I didn't tell my mother that I had lost yet another job. It was the last thing she needed in the middle of chemo and radiation. My itinerant employment had always worried her, and it was the last thing she needed to hear right now. You'd think that with my communications/theater major and 1.9 GPA, life would roll out the red carpet for me. But I just never knew what I was supposed to be *doing*, and I didn't know what my skills (none) or capabilities (none) were. My two sisters had had training and actual jobs: Therese was a CPA and a county manager, and Liz had a masters in adaptive physical education and loved teaching. My younger brothers were a sound engineer and a nurse anesthetist. These were the kinds of measurable, unambiguous, 9-5, Monday through Friday stability gigs my mother wanted for me. By the time I was 31, I'd gotten— and been fired or laid off from—seven or so jobs. But by this point, I was in my mid-forties and had supported myself for years writing and performing—although I think she was still worried I'd end up living in their basement.

My first job out of college was with K-tel International, makers of compilation albums like *20 Power Hits* and *Super Bad*. One of my coworkers did stand-up comedy and talked me into going to an open stage. I memorized three minutes of material - the time limit - and when I got onstage I panicked and immediately forgot two minutes of it. One that I remembered was, *"My name is Mary Jo Pehl. My father is an accountant, and my mother is a martyr."* Finally getting over her fear of my failure, my mother came to one of my shows. Right in the middle of the joke, I remembered she was in the audience. Once the audience laughed, she did too. After the show, I kind of apologized in a roundabout way. *It's just for fun, I'm just teasing.* But she was thrilled to be a character in my act, and she'd picked up some of the jargon. *You killed!* she said with some satisfaction but mostly relief. From then on she'd tell people: *She talks about me in her skit – I'm in her act.*

Enduring Love
McEwan, Ian
Starts out good (hot air balloon crash) but quit after about 100 pages.
Too much philosophizing. Did not like characters. He wrote "Cement
Gardens" which was also strange. Do not read any more by him.

Pilot's Wife
Shreve, Anita
9/10
Pilot lost in a plane crash. Wife learns of his double life.

In my mid-twenties, just as I was about to get fired from yet another job, I started to make a tiny bit of money doing comedy and the occasional essay for a community newspaper at ten dollars for 500 words. My parents didn't quite get how I cobbled together a living: daytime temp work for minimum wage and comedy gigs at night, driving two hours for 20 dollars. I didn't know how it was working either, but somehow I made it month to month. The unpredictable aggregation of freelance writing, acting, and comedy somehow turned out to be the steadiest employment I'd ever had.

Then I got hired as a writer on a television show produced in the Twin Cities in which the stars heckled old, bad movies. The local fandom turned the show into a cult phenomenon, and the show was picked up by cable channels. All of that escaped me at the time. All I knew was that I went to a 9-5, Monday-through-Friday job where I watched old movies and wrote jokes. And I got benefits.

My mother and I talked almost every Sunday morning, whether I was living across the country or just seven miles away in Minneapolis. One of those mornings, she asked about the job. It had been eight months since I'd been fired or laid off from a job, which was extraordinary. I gushed. *Mom,* I told her, *I'm good at something! I fit in! I'm using a skill set I didn't even know I had. I'm having so much fun! There's free pop in the fridge! We have benefits!*

My mother listened to me burble, and said, "Well, that'll all come crashing down around you."

Blue Shoe
Lamott, Ann
Divorced woman with 2 children, her looney mother. Story of her find-
ing out about deceased father's activities as a rounder. Had great reviews
but I found it a bit tiresome.

Finnegan's Week
Wambaugh, Joseph
Fiction involving illegal dumping of hazardous waste (San Diego to
Mexico) + the theft of 2000 pair of steel toe (navy?) shoes.

There was always that other shoe. It was a phrase she often dished out: *Just waiting for the other shoe to drop.* It comes from life in the overcrowded and ramshackle tenement buildings of late 19th-early 20th century New York, when everyone could hear the goings-on of everyone else through the thin walls. A person might take off their shoe and drop it to the floor, and a neighbor next door or below would wait for the sound of the other one. Don't get too excited or relieved about anything, don't take anything for granted because it's all just a big cosmic set-up, and the universe is just waiting *to pull the rug out from under you*, another one of her axioms.

Maybe I shouldn't have been so hard on her, considering I'd burned through seven or eight jobs by that point. But something in me snapped that day. I always went along to get along. I was always worried about how "sensitive" I might appear by having a reaction to anything. But this time I was mad, and it all just came out. "Maybe, but so what? Why can't I just enjoy it for what it is now? Who knows what will happen ever for any of us? Why can't you just be happy for me? I get benefits, for crying out loud!"

I hung up. We didn't speak for months after that.

Ride
Walton, David
Bus riders + the people + ordeals.
Man is in charge of teaching mentally challenged people
to ride bus on their own to get to jobs.
Made me uncomfortable + guilty.

Mom! Did you see this article?" I yelled. "About these 'bus groups'?"

I was in my broke and freeloading twenties and often stopped at my parents' house for coffee and their Sunday paper. When I was a kid, we got both the a.m. and p.m. editions of the Minneapolis daily, but oh, how I loved the thick Sunday edition. I'd lay the newspaper out on the floor, kneel, and prop myself up on my elbows with my butt stuck in the air and my face inches from the pages.

That morning there was an article in the Variety section about "bus clubs," people who rode the same commuter bus every day and formed tight-knit groups, sitting all together and squatting the same cluster of seats each morning and night. They gabbed nonstop on the ride into and back from the city. They knew one another's schedules and would be alarmed if a regular didn't get on the bus at the appointed time. If an unsuspecting commuter tried to sit in the claimed territory, they would be informed they had to sit elsewhere. They would celebrate birthdays, cutting a cake and distributing slices among themselves while the bus made its way downtown (Someone, I thought, wielding a sharp object on a giant, lurching city bus.) The camaraderie made my skin crawl.

My mother was somewhere in the house. I picture her in a robe, maybe bending over at the waist as she sorted a pile of laundry, since she couldn't crouch with her bad knees. I can still hear her voice ringing through the walls with an unhesitating response.

"Oh, gross!"

Neither of us were "joiners." She took the bus to her job downtown, and she always made sure she had a book. A book discouraged anyone from trying to strike up a conversation. The cliques on her bus irritated her no end. "They take over the whole bus like they own it!" she beefed, her eyes bugged out with annoyance. "Saving seats like it's grade school!"

"I'm afraid to even say good morning to anyone. They're going to try and suck me right into their little club." She snapped her fingers in a sort of exclamation point.

The Oprah Book Club irritated her on principle, even though there weren't any actual meetings with dreaded *other people*. She hated it if she just happened to want to read a certain book that ended up being part of the Book Club. It was just the very *idea* of a club.

Where The Heart Is
Letts, Billie
7/10
Oprah book – Baby born in Walmart store

My mother started water aerobics classes at a fitness center. There were cliques in the class too. She'd get to class early and stake out a claim in the pool, but other people would arrive and elbow past her so they could be by their pals. "In my mind I had carved out a clear space around me!" she huffed. But she never missed a class. Once the instructor announced that my mother was the best in the class at treading water. My mother had a smug split second of feeling not *average*, then the instructor went on to blithely explain that yes, the higher one's BMI, the easier it was to stay buoyant. My mother relayed the anecdote with a wry tilt to her mouth and that single-shoulder shrug. There was that other shoe.

S ome years Before Cancer, I was shocked to discover an audiobook of *The Secret* on my parents' kitchen countertop. Another Oprah pick and a huge bestseller, it's a self-help book based on the "law of attraction." It claims that you can visualize anything you desire by changing your thinking. I couldn't remember my mother ever reading a self-help book or any kind of positive-thinking manifesto. Unlike me, who'd read just about every self-improvement book there was.

"Mom! This is just—just *dumb!*" I sputtered after I read the description on the box.

She pursed her lips and did the one-shoulder shrug. "Who knows?"

"So if all the people in, oh, let's say Africa, read *The Secret*, their problems would be solved?" I asked.

She scoffed back. "Of course not! They can't read English!"

What was it she wanted to change with *The Secret*? Short legs? Weight? Averageness? Cancer?

Soft tinkling chimes echoed through the hospital as we held vigil at my mother's hospital bed in the middle of that night. In the darkness, my sister said quietly from across the room, "That means a baby's been born." Sometimes I wonder about that baby. They would be five, six, or seven years old by now.

My mother and I had had the exact same conversation over and over again over the years. I'd say to my mother, the same way every time: *Giving birth terrifies me. It's all…. so disgusting.* Childless my whole life, giving birth seemed apocryphal to me, despite billions of humans to the contrary.

Every single time my mother would respond: *Oh, but you forget about it right away.* I wasn't sure what that meant. Did that mean the instant the baby was placed in your arms? Or 50 years later, time being relative and all? Because I can hold a grudge for a long time. And in spite of *forgetting about it right away*, my mother managed to go into vivid and exacting details about each of her deliveries. To me, they were like scary campfire stories. All she needed was a flashlight under her chin and say in a sinister voice: *And then the baby crowned!*

And besides, MJ, millions of women have done it for millions of years, she'd say in her slightly exasperated way but with a little smile.

That doesn't make it right, I'd say righteously.

The exchange was almost ritualistic; the sameness was comforting. I really wanted to know about this exotic place called having children, and who knew better than my very own mother? I think what I really wanted to know was who my mother was. Questions I didn't know how to ask: *Who are you? Who were you? Before you met Dad? Before five kids? And as life happened to you?*

I'd ask, "If you had to do it all over again, would you have had children?"

"I tried so hard to be the perfect mother," my mother laughed. Her fingers fluttered in exasperation. She had five kids by the time she was 33. "All the other mothers in the neighborhood seemed to be doing it right," she said.

It was Christmas, and my mother had planned to recite the Nativity story to us kids to create a magical holiday tradition. She reverently launched into Joseph and the Virgin Mary on their way to Bethlehem, Mary great with child riding a donkey. Therese, who was only five, started to wail. "I want to ride a donkey!" My mother soldiered on and described Baby Jesus being born in a manger, and described it as being like a barn. Liz, four, started crying. "You always say you're going to take us to a farm, and you never do!"

"It all went to hell," she said, rolling her eyes.

Dreams of My Russian Summers
Makine, Andrei
I did not finish due to busy Xmas holiday.
Hard to get into but was interesting.

End In Tears
Rendell, Ruth
Gave it up about ½ way thru because I was unable to keep track of people + things. So many holiday things to side-track me. English author.

F orty and firmly ensconced in middle-age, I realized my mother's worst nightmare: I moved back in with my parents. My mother could get behind my peripatetic freelance life so long as it kept me from having to move home again. But there I was.

I'd worked for the television show almost seven years, the longest I'd ever had a job in my whole life, and I was out of a job when it got cancelled. I sold or gave away almost everything I owned, moved out of my apartment and traveled on and off for a year. The plan was that I'd stay with my parents when I got back while I figured out the next chapter of my life. My dream was to move to New York. In the meantime, I slept on a daybed in the corner of my father's office in the basement, living out of suitcases and boxes stacked against the wall. I sent out letters and emails, trying to find a job in New York, while I listened to my mother and father going about their business on the floor above. I'd known them for 40 years, and they must have always had their own lives. But back under the same roof with them, as a full-grown adult, I was like an infant with my own version of object impermanence. I was kind of surprised to realize that my mother and father had existed beyond my sight, living lives that I knew nothing about.

I'd come upstairs for breakfast in the morning. My mother would be standing at the big window over the sink, in her robe with coffee mug in hand. That window was her front-row seat to the goings-on in the neighborhood. Their house was on the corner of a busy intersection in a bustling neighborhood, kitty-corner from a dingy, cigarette smoke-laden mini-mart and across the street from a city bus stop. A few doors down was Sandy's, a divey supper club from whence you could smell the greasy hamburgers on nights when the wind was right.

My mother loved it all. She surveyed her corner of the world from the big kitchen window as my father sat at the table with his breakfast and the daily paper.

"Oh, geez. Look at that guy," she'd mutter about someone walking by. "Check out Mr. Cool."

A "Mr. Cool" could be any guy 20-80 years old who, say, might be wearing a t-shirt with a rock-band logo. And/or smoking. And/or driving a car less than 20 years old in a color other than black or gray. A sip from her mug, and with a sigh, she'd concur with herself. "Yep. There goes Mr. Cool." Maybe she'd start preparing the night's dinner, like meatloaf. Taking off her wedding ring and putting it on the windowsill, she'd plunge into the raw hamburger, breadcrumbs, and seasonings with her bare hands to mix it all together. *It just mixes better this way.*

The squishing sounds punctuated her observations. "Yep. Mr. Cool." *Missssster* drawn out as she shook her head. *Squish, pause, squish, pause,* as her eyes narrowed at all the Mr. Cools in the world passing by.

A detective series my mother read featured a protagonist who probably would have been one of her "Mr. Cools." She was all over the place with her opinion of him - and the spelling of his name.

A Morning For Flamingos
James Lee Burke
Cajun detective in New Orleans out to catch a killer drug dealer who killed his partner and left him for dead. "Dave Robicheaux"

Swan Lake
James Lee Burke
8/10
Dave Robecieu myst always good

Jolie Blon's Bounce
James Lee Burke
7/10
Character Dave Robinshauer after killer of 16 yr old girl gets very violent.

Black Cherry Blues
James Lee Burke
7/10
Ex-cop Dave Robicheaux (Louisiana) series with Montana connections. Also involves his ex partner Clete, also an ex-cop gone bad. Clete is a dichotomy of good and bad.

Crusader's Cross
James Lee Burke
6.5/10
Hero marries nun (no final vows), deep south, serial killer.
Getting tired of hero Dave Robicheaux behavior.

Sunset Limited
James Lee Burke
6/10
Dave Robicheau (ongoing personality) cop in Louisiana in tale of man
crucified 30 years earlier.
His daughter, (?) comes back to find who is responsible.

Tin Roof Blow Down
James Lee Burke
8/10
Dave Robicheaux novel. New Orleans after Katrina mystery

Months passed as I bunkered in the basement, and I got more and more antsy. My grand plans for New York just couldn't seem to pan out. I sent out résumés by the truckload; I tried to work any connections I had. Nothing. My mother and father were patient, but I was going stir-crazy. My mother corrected me every time I referred to my living quarters as "the basement." The nomenclature was demeaning after so much time and money fixing it up. "Lower level, M.J.—lower level."

The Fourth Hand
Irving, John
5/10
TV reporter loses his hand in a 30 second episode all filmed to a lion in a cage. Usually like his stuff but thought this was kind of dumb.

One night I was sitting with her in the recliners upstairs. My mother laid her book in her lap and took off her reading glasses.

"Have you ever thought of being a news anchor on CNN?" Her fingers skimmed her chin for goat hairs.

I put down my book, baffled. "No. Why?"

"Well, all those anchors have such nice skin - and you have a beautiful complexion!"

I don't know what happened in the years between *it'll all come crashing down* and *you could be an anchor for a major news outlet!* Maybe she'd started thinking anything was possible. And the fact that all those news anchors probably got good benefits did not escape her.

I sat in the car in a grocery store parking lot in Austin, sobbing to my mother on the phone. Alan and I had moved to Austin together after a seven-month long distance romance, and a few months later we decided to get married. I was panicking. I'd never sought marriage advice from my mother because I never thought I'd need it. I never thought any man would ever want to give me his seed, even just recreationally. I was 47. I'd had relationships here and there, but I'd just stopped thinking I'd ever get married. I figured I wasn't thin enough, beautiful enough, smart enough, anything enough to be anything but "just friends" with a man.

"What the hell am I doing?" I wailed. I always second-, third-, or eleventh-guessed myself about everything, whether it be marriage or choosing a brand of toilet paper. "What if we get divorced?" I wailed. It would be Alan's fifth marriage but, he was quick to clarify, I would be only his fourth wife. He had to walk me through the math: he'd married one woman twice. My mother didn't bat an eye: "Well," she supposed, "he still believes in love."

Maybe she secretly thought he was a savage, but she liked Alan. Even if she'd demanded to see his driver's license the first time she met him. He'd come to Minnesota for the first time in our long-distance relationship and was picking up my car and apartment keys from my parents. I was out of town, had left the car with them so it wouldn't be parked on a city street for several weeks, and Alan would pick me up at the airport. The way he told it, she demanded his license, muttering "I don't like doing this - I don't even know you." She put on her reading glasses and scanned him up and

down, comparing him to the photo on his license and finally relin-
quishing the keys.

"So what?!" my mother said.

The weariness in her voice was lost on me at the time. She was
in San Francisco with her sister, my aunt Marlene, who was un-
dergoing treatment for skin cancer. My mother was helping with
the house and laundry and cooking, and just being there for her
sister. And there was shopping. Marlene loved bargains as much
as my mother, and it was probably very therapeutic for both of
them. But my mother was exhausted. Marlene was prickly, and my
mother once whispered over a phone call that Marlene only talked
about her shih tzu, Charlie. Marlene was telling everyone that
she wouldn't have been able to manage the whole ordeal without
Charlie. *Charlie this, Charlie that! While I'm folding her laundry and
cleaning the toilet!* My mother half laughed and half sighed. *And he's
a really stupid dog, too!*

"M.J.-" Again with that sigh of hers. Not exactly irritated and not
unkind - maybe just a kind of knowing. "Millions of people get
divorced all the time. You'd live."

In the background I could hear my aunt. "Oh, Charlie! Good
puppy! What would I do without you!?" I could feel my mother's
jaw clenching over the phone.

"You have to give it a shot, don't you?"

My self-absorption knew no bounds, demanding my mother pre-
dict my future while her sister was dying.

Back When We Were Grownups
Tyler, Anne
8/10
53 yr old woman "Beck" married to a divorced man with 3 daughters.
They have 1 daughter + he's killed in a car accident. She runs a home +
holds parties for income.

Special Circumstances
Siegel, Sheldon
8/10
Goes through trial of an attorney accused of double murder of attorneys
in his large office – he is defended by an ex-priest now divorce attorney.

It was the summer after fifth grade, and I'd found my sister's copy of *Love Story*. I wasn't even supposed to be in her bedroom, but there it was, among all the clothes and magazines and Barbra Streisand albums strewn on the floor. A slim paperback with the iconic Robert Indiana typeface on the cover, I grabbed it and it went to the couch in the rec room. My father, an accountant for a flooring store, had stapled carpet samples on the walls in a funky patchwork. (I thought this was so cool, so creative - only later in life did I realize it probably muffled the sounds of kids fighting and the television blaring constantly.) I finished the book in one sitting, and I collapsed in sobs on the couch. I called my mother at work bawling.

"What? What's the matter? M.J.? What's going on?" she hissed, panicking but trying to remain professional.

I wailed *"Mom! What can you say about a 25-year-old girl who died?"*

"What are you talking about?" she hissed.

"Lovvvvvvve…. (hiccup) Storeeeeeeeeeeee…!"

Her voice lowered, and the words came out clipped. "I can say never call me at work unless one of you is bleeding or dead." Click.

My mother took me to the local jeweler to get her wedding band re-sized for my beefy finger. The shop was a repurposed, old-style, barn-shaped Dairy Queen, and ghosts of Dilly Bars past swirled in the bright lights and sparkling diamonds on display. A loupe on her face, the jeweler found two letters on the inscription inside the band. After more than 50 years on my mother's hand, only the "F" and "r" of the word *forever* in teeny scrolled lettering could be made out. The jeweler measured my finger and tucked the half-inch wide gold band into a small velvet bag along with instructions for resizing. My mother had instructions too: "Don't go in the pool with it - chlorine is very hard on gold."

"The band is so wide - at some point the skin under it will peel off. Just once. It won't hurt."

"Ewwwww…," I moaned, as if she was describing scenes from the film *Saw*.

"I think you'll live."

Amateur Marriage
Tyler, Anne
7/10
Couple married quickly because of WWII. Real mismatch.

See No Evil
Bland, E.
6/10
*Woman cop engaged to paramedic, all kinds of troubles including stalker
of her family & her snitch (neighborhood drunk). Not real exciting.*

And one Friday afternoon, my parents drove Alan and me
to the courthouse in St. Paul to get married. My father
drove, the way he always did when we went anywhere as
kids. My mother in the passenger seat let her left arm stretch out
and dangle behind the driver's seat. I used to play with her hand
as it hung there, tracing the half-moons of her smooth, oval nails
with my own stumpy fingers and nails chewed to the quick. I'd spin
the gold wedding ring round and round her finger as her elegant
fingers fluttered to emphasize something she might have been saying to my father. Sometimes the ring spun more easily than others,
depending on what weight she was at.

I was again in the backseat that afternoon with my brand-new husband and my parents in the front seats, as if they were driving us to
prom and we weren't a newly married couple nearing their 50s. We
headed back to their house for a small family picnic. My mother's
left hand rested on the back of the driver's seat like it always did.
She'd given me her wedding ring and now wore a new ring my
father had given her. My sister had soaped "Just Married" on the
back windshield and had tied both cowboy and snow boots to the

bumper in a nod to both our cultures. Cars honked. Alan and I playfully wrestled our hands across the seat and clinked our wedding bands - his came from Walmart - and laughed.

"Oh, cut it out, you two!" my mother said. I didn't know if she was smiling or rolling her eyes, but I suspect it was the latter. Too much hokey for her.

Mattie Spencer's Journal
Sandra Dallas
8/10
Young bride and groom homesteading in flat lands of Colo.
Very sweet + easy reading.

Hemlock Boy
Catherine Coulter
3/10
FBI husband wife team with sister who owns valuable paintings.
Junior high level.

My mother always waved away any questions about other boyfriends before she met my father. There was a shoebox of letters from Joe Manning, with whom she corresponded while he was in the service. She called them love letters, but when I read them, it seemed more like pen pals. But maybe there was an intensity to the banal day-to-day that escaped me, that might have been known only to them. Then there was Bob Duerr, a local celebrity herpetologist and reptile keeper at a local small zoo. He had a popular exhibit at the Minnesota State Fair, Bob's Snake House, and was a regular, along with his snakes, on the local kids' television show *Lunch With Casey*.

"Mother!" I would teasingly bemoan. "I could have been the scion of a herpetological, serpent, vermin empire!" I was barely getting by as a comedian, and I was probably thinking how it might have been a leg up in my career - a real "in" in show biz. But no, you had to marry an accountant."

The little curl to the corners of her lips. "Oh, M.J.! One date! It was one date! Maybe two."

If I had married him, I wouldn't have gotten the five of you.

Then a little shrug, a quick little raise of the shoulders where you didn't know if maybe that would have been preferable. Mustn't get *too* carried away with any sort of sentimentality.

I'd asked my mother about marriage.

Capital M-A-R-R-I-A-G-E. This was long before I met Alan, and it seemed downright apocryphal that a couple would have anything to discuss three weeks into a relationship, much less nearly six decades.

"What do you talk about all day? Every day? For that many years?" I'd asked, eyes huge with mystification. It was another secret of the universe my mother held, having been married to my father for fifty-plus years. *Well...* my mother puckered her chin in thought.

You talk about your day... you make plans for the weekend... there's always something with the house, like a broken garbage disposal or something... sometimes you fight. And there's always the kids to talk about.

There were five of us, so I'm sure my parents were never at a loss.

When Alan and I decided to get married, I did my homework. I checked out Stephanie Coontz's massive *Marriage, a History: How Love Conquered Marriage* from the library. The very thing of books themselves make sense to me: pages squared off and sentences plumb to the page. Black ink crisply delineated against white paper. One sentence leading to another, and the next, and the next; words marching single file with information. I finished the book like it was an owner's manual to the next phase of my life, and I was ready.

A few months after our wedding, I heard Alan coming down the walk after his work day. I got excited when he came home, and I was kind of giddy and nervous when he walked in the door, like we were still dating. That afternoon, before the door even shut behind him and completely randomly and unprompted, I blurted, "I tried a new variety of Lean Cuisine today. And I really like it."

My mother would have been proud that I was keeping the love alive.

The Turnaround
Pelecanos, George
0
Boring. Quit after about half.

Bloody Roller Blues
Jeffrey Deaver
Mystery which got a bit boring. Movie being made in MO with story of a stuntman.

Story of Lucy Gault
Trevor, William
6/10
Nine year old girl runs away from Ireland home to avoid moving to England with wealthy parents. They think she died in ocean + leave. 1920's and don't find out she's alive. It gets long + maudlin.

A lan and I adopted a shaggy little black mutt from a dog rescue organization in Austin. He was like a Mad Max car, an assemblage of dog parts with no rhyme or reason. But we fell madly in love with Seymour, and we might have gone a little overboard. We were like excited, first-time parents: we congratulated ourselves on his intelligence when he remembered where his treats were kept. We sent a cheek swab from a Skymall DNA kit to find out what breeds he might be. Alan and I began referring to each other as "Mom" and "Dad." Every morning I'd grab Seymour's leash and say, "Go tell Dad we're going for a walk!" Alan and I would delight when Seymour would dash to the general vicinity of Alan, then dash back to me, eager to get a move on, and out the door we'd go.

Don't Let's Go To The Dogs Tonight
Fuller, Alexandra
9.5/10
Autobiography of an African childhood.

Black Dog
Booth, Stephen
6/10
English author; murder of 15 year old girl (rich) in small village; moved slow.

Sick Puppy
Hiaason, Carl
(no rating)
Involves litterbugs in FLA. with past gove skink efforts to save + island
from big builders + corrupt officials.

All this fawning and fussing over Seymour took place in the privacy of our own home, 1200 miles away from my mother's gimlet eye. I'd always loved animals, and she could get a little eye-rolly about my *bless the beasts and the children (but mostly the beasts)* attitude. She once said offhandedly that blue jays were mean birds. I was pre-teen or so, and I started crying. *They're just trying to live their life, Mom!* I'd cry, practically beating my breast. I rescued tiny tree frogs from the driveway and repatriated them to the woods behind the house. I said silent prayers for road kill as we drove past the carcasses, hoping that they didn't suffer and that their raccoon or possum families could find closure. I was distraught when horses got injured on the old Westerns I watched on television. My mother asked tartly, "But you don't care about the humans?" I didn't quite know how to explain that the humans had brought it on themselves, and horses were innocent victims.

M y mother said *no* when I asked her if I should come home for the biopsy surgery. *Absolutely not.* Just as I'd hoped. Flying back to Minnesota would have been making a fuss, and a fuss would be acknowledging it might be serious. Ergo: no fuss made, it all goes away.

Like my mother's instructions to us about the mean kids when we were in grade school. *Ignore them. Don't let them see you cry on the bus - wait til you get in the house.* Ignore it. *Don't give cancer the satisfaction of reacting. You'll only encourage it.*

So Alan and I went to the movies instead. It was a typically hot and glaringly bright day, and it would be a distraction, and we were the only people in the theater. Denzel Washington flashed across the screen. Too cute to be trusted, as if the outcome of the biopsy were up to him.

My phone buzzed, and I crawled over Alan to take it out in the hall, accidentally stepping in the popcorn bag he'd left on the floor.

"Oh, hi. Okay…" Mike said in a measured tone. "Well, it's cancer."

"How can they know that? They can't know that!" I hissed, like I was being choked.

"They do," he sighed. "They just do."

I clambered next to Alan back in the auditorium. "We have to go. It's cancer," I hissed. I can't remember what the movie was, and I have no idea how it ends.

A Virtuous Woman
Gibbons, Kaye
Blinking Jack Stokes marries Ruby (20 years younger) after her disastrous marriage. She dies of lung cancer.

M y mother had a question for the oncologist: *why me?* *We don't know,* he said.

Just before Christmas of that year, I moved home once again, but I had a mission this time. My mother would be starting chemo and radiation, and I volunteered to be the on-site manager. I would track appointments and prescriptions, drive her to clinics and doctors' offices, and help around the house so it wouldn't all fall on my father. I didn't hesitate a moment to go to Minnesota in the dead of winter. I didn't have children that needed looking after, I could do my writing work from anywhere, and the comedy group I was touring with was on a break.

The cancer could be managed in lists and tasks that could be checked off a list, such as packing an enormous *Costco* tote bag with a comforter, books, snacks, and bottled water for her long chemo appointments. I tucked the comforter around her as my mother dozed in a brown recliner in the chemo stall at the clinic and situated crackers and lavender essential oil for nausea on the table next to her. I kept a notebook of appointments, doctors' conversations, and what she ate each day, and reported to my siblings in daily email updates. I was going to be good at *this* job, dammit. My siblings took turns filling the refrigerator, getting my father out of the house so he wouldn't hover too much, and taking my mother out to lunch or shopping or visiting friends when she had the energy.

On the way to appointments in my parents' old oafish minivan, my mother's hand would rest on the back of the driver's seat. She talked. She talked about her girlhood, her brothers and sisters, and her mother, who died suddenly when my mother was 24, just after I'd been born. Her aunt and uncle's farmhouse, of which we had many photographs in albums and on the walls over the years. And the story I'd heard over and over again as if she needed to exorcise it: I was about three years old, and my parents didn't realize I had significant hearing loss. My mother took me to the doctor - and her face always scrunched up at this point - and the male doctor said to her, "Mother, how could you have let this happen?" The part that gets me is that she didn't even have a name. And she was the one who "let it happen."

I don't remember much of these conversations. I was planning on listening soon. My ears would cloud up with anxiety about traffic and parking and getting her to the clinic on time and the duty of keeping her alive goddamn it. I was planning on listening soon, just as soon as this thing was under control.

Zorro
Isabel Allende
Lost interest (boring) – quit on page 131

Bombay Ice
Forbes, Leslie
Read about 50 pages – story of India – could not get interested.

These Granite Islands
Stonich, Sarah
Read 76 pages and could not get interested. Quit.

Me—absolutely *no* interest in food. Can you believe it?" My mother's eyes got big, and she tilted a corner of her mouth as she marveled at this. She was tired all the time, and she'd lost interest in most everything: eating, reading, and removing unwanted facial hair. We stocked the refrigerator with Ensure and chicken noodle soup, about the only things she could eat. Books started stacking up on the coffee table, waiting for her to feel better. The recliner began to be outsized around her as she shrank. The book that was always in her lap usually sat there unopened. In an ordeal comprised mostly of *worsts,* this seemed like the worst of it.

"The doctor is actually telling me to eat more! That has never ever happened in my whole life!" My mother sputtered a weak little laugh. *Now if I can just keep it off.*

Starvation Lake
Gruley, Brian
Read about 80 pages – too much about hockey for me.

Skeletons At The Feast
Bohjalian, Chris
8/10
Last year of WWII. Germans & Jews trying to get to
Brit and American rather than the Russians.

T wo months after I'd started The Dorothy Pehl Cancer Management Project, it was time to go back to Austin. I mentally dusted my palms together: *Chemo and radiation all wrapped up! Done and done! All good!*

Back in Texas, I didn't know what to do with myself. Aimless and preoccupied, it seemed to take every ounce of energy I had to be completely helpless. I did laundry, walked the dog, went to the grocery store, watched movies, vacuumed the rugs, circled classes in the community ed catalog, all stuff of my regular life. But I was just killing time until my mother might call and announce everything was back to normal and then we could all carry on as before.

I went to the library, getting six, seven, eight books at a time. Novels, enormous nonfiction tomes, canonical children's books I'd never read, fad diet books (*might as well work on self-improvement while Mom gets better*). But I'd start a book and just couldn't concentrate. I would start worrying about the other books patiently waiting for me, as if they felt slighted. And I wouldn't admit that I needed reading glasses. I held books with my arms fully extended in front of me, moving the book left and right like a machine gunner, trying to find the exact right position to be able to see the words. Books would get returned to the library, one or two pages read, and then I'd start all over again with a whole new set of books. One broiling Texas day, I had so many books piled in my arms they toppled over and landed in a heap of splayed spines and crumpled pages on the sizzling tar. I sat down and cried.

Twelfth Card
Jeffrey Deaver
Returned before reading. Could not get into!

Bonus Army
Dickenson & Allen
Non-fic - looked good but did not read -
looked like more work than I was willing - due back

Dark Horse
Hoag, Tami
Had a good review but just don't like her books -
returned after over 100 pages.

I was back in Minnesota the summer after her chemo and radiation, back in the basement bedroom. One night, I poked my head in the doorway of my parents' bedroom to say goodnight. For as long as I could remember, my mother loved to crawl in bed in the early evening and watch television. And by "early evening," I believe other people might call it *late afternoon.* There was always a TV in their bedroom, and this one had a large flat-screen on the dresser, which was about ten feet from another, even bigger, flat screen mounted on the wall in the "official" TV room. My parents' bed was huge, too—two separate single mattresses created a king-size bed. Each mattress had its own articulating bed frame, like a hospital bed, so each of them could position themselves to their liking. A lot of family business was conducted in the master bedroom. You'd stand in the doorway or sit on the edge of the bed to discuss something with my mother, a short, drowsy Godfather propped up in her bendy bed. With the covers pulled up to her chin and her arms tucked out of sight, she was just a shadowy face and a mound under the blankets in the glow of the screen.

But this night there was no mound, no rounded form under the bedspread. She was just a wan face and a weak smile and a quiet "Good night, Mairzy Doats."

Still, she would talk about the pants in the closet that she could finally fit into. Pants she'd outgrown but now could fit back into, or the aspirational pants, those she'd bought in a smaller size to motivate her.

"I'm down to a size 14. I haven't seen that since I got married."

Maybe that's why I thought she wasn't *actually dying*. If she could envision a future in size 14 pants, then I could—and would—too.

And once again: "I just don't want to gain it all back."

A s my father and I sorted through the closets, we found her tiny black Singer sewing machine. It was tucked in a corner in its own tote box no bigger than a lawyer's attache. The machine was as basic as they get: it only did straight stitches, save for a complicated button-holer attachment. This was the machine my mother had made her wedding dress on, and through the years she used it to let out or take in clothes, depending on the fortunes of her weight. She also made clothes for me from patterns that came in my size or could be enlarged, or she modified her clothes or those of a plump neighbor for me to wear. I was always larger than my sisters so there were no such things as hand-me-downs, and I was "hard to buy for"—I got to an age where the Chubbies sizes at Sears were too juvenile, and Lane Bryant at that time carried only unfashionable, polyester clothes for older women.

My mother was always looking for a way to keep her hands busy to *try to stay out of the food*, as she put it. There were always capital letters in the way my mother said The Food, and it was never just *food*, it was always THE food. My parents took up decoupage, a major art movement of 1970s suburbia. Old timey art prints were singed along the edges as if they'd been salvaged from a fire, then shellacked onto a faux-dilapidated piece of wood. There were decoupage prints all over our house and all the other houses in the neighborhood.

There was my mother's knitting and crocheting period. I was about eight years old when I asked her to knit mittens for a Salvation Army bell ringer at the Target store we went to. The man at the kettle was blind and without gloves in the raw Minnesota winter, and it agonized me. I begged my mother to make mittens for him and we made another trip back to Target a week later. My mother made me deliver the mittens to the man myself. I didn't want to. I was always anxious around people, especially in awkward situations and *every* situation was awkward. I wanted my mother to handle it. She'd know what to say and do. I approached tentatively and put the mittens in his hands. He felt them and I murmured that my mother had made them.

"Oh, great," he said. "More mittens." He tossed them aside - maybe there was a bench behind him. "Everybody gives me mittens. Got plenty of mittens." And he went on ringing his bell, barehanded.

Tenderness of Wolves
Penny, Stef
9/10
1867 Canada myst. + tale. Hard winter. Very good.

Cold Pursuit
Parke, T. Jefferson
Boring – quit halfway through.

Cold Mountain
Frazier, Charles
8/10
Simple story of man's journey home after wounded in Civil War.
The people he comes in contact with (good + evil)

I walked back to my mother waiting at the car, embarrassed and holding back tears, as per usual. My mother shrugged a shoulder, draped an arm over the passenger seat and backed out of the parking space.

Well, I'm not a very good knitter anyway.

Zero. The absolute rock bottom for my mother. People could be zeros: *He's just a big zero,* she'd say about someone she didn't like. Nil, a cipher, insignificant, devoid of any redeeming qualities. With books, it wasn't enough to just dislike them or stop reading them. She made a point of giving them a big old goose egg on her scale of 1-10. Her plump, round "0"s seem so defiant in her handwriting.

Dubious Legacy
Wesley, Mary
0/10
English - could not get into it.

Quite A Year for Plums
White, Bailey
0/10
A bunch of goofy people in the South. Bird watchers.
Mary Olson loved. I could not get into. Read 100 pages.

Freedomland
Price, Richard
0/10
Quit after about 75 pages – difficult reading using lots of street slang.
Story of woman whose car was hijacked + her child was sleeping in back
seat. He also wrote Clockers which I didn't get.

Hornet's Nest
Patricia Cornwell
0/10
Quit after almost half book read.
Very disjointed newspaper reporter & woman detective. Dumb.

Judas Child
O'Connell, Carol
0/10
Quit after about ½ way. Mystery that seemed dumb + drawn out.
Could not work up any feelings for the main people.

Long Road Home
Gay, William
0/10
Quit in less than 50 pages. Did not like the characters + liked the author
even less.
Long windy + self indulgent descriptions that seemed so trite + like he
was trying soooo hard.

My mother seemed to be holding steady after the winter's chemo and radiation treatments, and Alan, Seymour and I drove back to Minnesota that summer for a visit. Once again, we were in the queen-size bed in the basement room. One morning I came upstairs with Seymour to take him for a walk. My mother was standing at the sink in sweat pants and a bra. She had abandoned any sense of modesty at that point. "Oh, who cares," she said with a weak smile and a wave of her fingers. Her eyes were flat and tired those days, but every morning she got up and got going, even if it was propping herself against the sink in her bra to wash strawberries. I squeezed past her to get to the coffee maker, and rubbed her upper back. It was soft and smooth, belying its 78 years.

I took Seymour's leash and chirped, "Go tell Grandma we're going for a walk." I can still see my mother, gripping the rim of the sink and staring out the window. She snapped, "I am not that dog's grandmother."

My face burned. *Of course she wasn't Seymour's grandmother. You didn't need a Skymall catalog DNA test to tell you that – all you had to do was compare their photos!* I thought as I tried not to cry and hustle out the door. I'd only wanted to make her laugh. I'd thought things were becoming normal again. I'd only seen what I wanted to see. Things would never be normal, whatever that was, whatever we thought it had been.

Still, when I went to write her obituary, it was all I could do to not list Seymour as her "grand-dog." Maybe it would have been retribution for all the Cheesecake Accusations. I wanted to get the last word in.

Chemo and radiation, along with the blood thinner medication my mother had been on for years, made my mother's skin raw at points, especially where her thighs rubbed together. It was extremely painful, and she was prescribed painkillers and had to have the wounds dressed by a visiting nurse. The painkillers made her dopey and without an appetite. We thought this was just a bump in the road since chemo and radiation seemed to be holding the cancer at bay. We were impatient: my mother should have been trying harder not to die.

Maybe they're just doing the best they can.

My mother's voice wafted through my brain as I stood in line at the grocery store. It was a couple of weeks after the funeral, weeks of fog and listlessness, and I began to cry as the person couldn't decide between paper and plastic. I'd shuffled to the grocery store in slippers and sweatpants. Also sans brassiere. I hadn't had the wherewithal to manage the three little hooks. I had to conserve my energy to secure a pint of Ben and Jerry's. And there, in an Austin HEB, I was the person I would have huffed about.

"Oh, please - how much trouble would it have been to put on shoes? Or foundation garments at the very least," I'd beef.

I was often up in arms about someone or something. It was up to me to save the world from people who couldn't get their shit together, wearing pajamas in public or holding their eating utensils like barbarians, and I was often vocal about it with my mother. We could not give these people a free pass. We were the thin righteous line between orderliness and anarchy.

Maybe that's all they could manage today, she'd say when I was in high dudgeon. *Who knows what's going on with them right now.*

Maybe they're doing the best they can.

It took me so long to understand that my mother had done the best she could. Everything she'd come with, her original factory settings, and everything she'd learned in her life before my father, before my siblings and me. I suppose she wanted something different for me, a something she could only guess at through her own lens.

D id my mother hear my cheesecake confession that night? The hearing is the last to go, so they say, and she'd had the ears of a bat when I was growing up. She knew when any of us were in the kitchen - especially me. She could detect exactly what I was getting into by the slightest rustle of a package being opened or an exhalation of a Tupperware lid or the soft pop of the suction on the refrigerator door when I pulled on it. Oh, how I tried to be stealthy. In my recollection I am moving along the hardwood floors into the kitchen like Mission Impossible-Tom Cruise-not-tripping-the-infrared-lights-in-the-museum. I knew just how many creaks there were in the stairs. How to keep the flatware from rattling as I eased the drawer open. How many motions it would take to get the yellow Nestle chocolate chips bag from the cupboard and under my shirt, and how many steps it took to get to the mudroom and hide it in the pocket of my winter coat hanging on the hook. But there was always a point when I'd hear her holler from her bed, "What are you doing in there?" Even now, all grown up and well into middle age, having lived in many apartments and houses, I still have a sense of unease going into my own kitchen. I hear it somewhere deep in my bones: "Are you looking for something?"

Hidden Prey
Sandford, John
6/10
Lucas Davenport in Duluth + the Iron Range –
these books are getting old to me.

Snow Flower + The Secret Fan
See, Lisa
8/10
Chinese foot binding.

Midsummer Malice
Lake, M.D.
5/10
Peggy O'Neil mystery – show boat – woman sells baby.

Gone Baby Gone
Lehane, Dennis
7/10
So-so -- not as good as later one he wrote. Children kidnapping story
– cops taking small children who are neglected, starved + beaten + give
them to good families.

Evidence Against Her
Rob Forman Dew
7/10
Very different-seemed to go nowhere but interesting characters. Takes
place in late 1800s with three babies born the same day to brothers + a
close friend.

M y mother declared she did not trust people who didn't talk to their babies.

I didn't know what she meant. A "sleep with one eye open" kind of mistrust? Such people were more likely to rob a bank?

No! Nooooo. Of course not! Complete with an eyeroll and a loud "pffffft!"

You have to talk to babies. They want to hear your voice. How else do you get to know who they are?

My mother was soft and tender with her grandchildren, and she was so short she didn't have to crouch to be at a child's level and look them in the face. She would enfold any one of the grandkids in a luxuriously fleshy embrace, her beautifully pendulous arms wrapping them in a soft hug, even if she'd just seen the same kids an hour before. It didn't matter if it was a strapping nephew who had to bend over to be hugged, or the squirmiest toddler. A distraught or tantruming kid would melt as she soothed them against her pillowy body.

The ones who are the hardest to love are the ones who need it most.

To watch her talking to infants was like witnessing more of her magic. It didn't matter whose baby: she would often help herself to a baby at any gathering, with that assuredness that long-time mothers have. A baby never fussed or cried in my mother's arms. My mother would hold the infant just so, its head cradled in her palm and its tiny body resting on her forearm, with her other hand cupping the tiny diapered bottom. This way could angle the baby to lean her lovely face into the child's. She'd ask the baby questions in a low, earnest voice. The baby would try hard to focus on her face and coo and flail its tiny limbs in response. Like they were the only two people in the world.

Wish You Well
D. Baldacci
9/10
Different from his usual mystery type. Story of young girl and boy in late 1930s sent to live with great grandmother along with comatose mother. They live in W. Virginia mountains and eek out a living.

Another World
Pat Barker
5/10
Dysfunctional family includes grandfather 101 yr. Old (killed his brother during WWI), husband and wife each with child from earlier marriage-one child together. All characters were mean spirited and I realized I didn't like any of them.

Doohickey
Pete Dexter
6/10
Grandfather who fakes his death to get grandson
to help market his many small inventions.

Red, White + Blue
Isaacs, Susan
8/10
FBI agent (Wyoming) meets reporter. Starts out with history of when
great great grandparents came to U.S. + where siblings parted + went to
far corners of U.S. They shared great great grandparents but never knew
it. Anti-semitic people involved.

Final Judgment
Patterson, Richard North
6/10
Attorney comes home after 20 years to defend her niece who is really her
daughter of charge of murder. Her father, grandfather of suspect is really
the guilty party.

I imagine my mother talking to me like when she'd had me. She'd labored alone in a hospital room, as with all my siblings, in the days before fathers were allowed in the delivery room. She'd had no idea what she was going to get with me or my two sisters or two brothers. All us wolves.

I was such a snob about my parents' television choices, and some of the schlocky novels and trope-y best-selling detective series in my mother's book files. But I also came across books that I would have found too daunting to even attempt. I might have had them on my shelves, thinking I'd get around to reading them, but in the meantime, I could pretend I was well-read. I would edge them out just a touch past the more plebeian books on my bookshelf to subliminally draw the eye in a pathetic attempt to impress people. But they'd never be cracked open. My mother, on the other hand, gave them a go.

East of Eden
Steinbeck, John
9/10
600 pages. Very good.

Wakefield
Andrei Codrescu
NO. Could not get interested.

Yiddish Policeman's Union
Michael Chabon
About 50 pages and hard reading

The Hours
Michael Cunningham
Three stories that intertwine. It took awhile to get into but very good author. Virginia Wolf was part of the book.

Falling Man
Don DeLillo
Read about ½ and still did not get it!

Justice
Dominick Dunne
7/10
Non-fiction of crimes, trials + punishment including actual accounts
Mendez Brothers + O.J. Very good but got a bit long.

Jar City
Indridason, Arnalidason
Gave up at about ¾ the way thru – too much work – translated.

The Widow Killer
Kohout, Pavel
Translated from Czech to English. Takes place near end of WWII with
occupation of Third Reich in Czech.
Very violent and I'm not sure if I liked it.

Girl With Dragon Tattoo
Larsson, Steig
8/10
Very good – hard to get into – Swedish author.

My mother said, "I guess I thought I'd never actually die." We were again in the TV room. Judge Judy was adjudicating a disagreement between roommates. It was chemo and radiation season for my mother, and I remember the sky's hostile lavender color, typical of a Minnesota winter. It was likely the only thing she was thinking about, but I thought we had been distracting her. We were following a plan, goddammit. Appointments. Stocked refrigerator and nutritional beverages and browbeating her into eating. We'd never even asked her how she felt about the plan. I must have also thought she'd never die too. All we had to do was keep kicking the can down the road. She gave a little snort laugh when she said it.

Sixteen months after the diagnosis, my mother died.

It was probably in that half-second I hadn't been thinking about her. It was my first horseback riding lesson in Austin, something I'd been wanting to do for ages and I thought it would take my mind off *things*. I'd managed to get up on the horse and it plucked its way through a scrubby Hill Country trail. I remember clearly the strange, fleeting moment my mother wasn't occupying all the lobes of my brain. It must have been the thing that people meant by *being in the moment*. But just as instantaneously, thoughts of her whiplashed back into my head.

When I got back to my car and cellphone, Liz had called four times. I called back, and she said in her typical measured tone, "Mom was admitted to the hospital this afternoon. You need to come as soon as you can."

I asked no questions, hung up, and set about obeying, as I always did with my sisters. I began driving down the country road and called back. "Is she still alive?"

Liz hesitated. "She's unresponsive. Just get home."

My constant worrying was supposed to have been a talisman, but the shoe dropped in that eighth of a moment when I wasn't.

Portrait in Sepia
Isabel Allende
8/10
Daughter and grand-daughter descendants of
Chinese and Chilean ancestry.

The last professional family photo we'd had was in the late 1970s. The seven of us staggered down a curving staircase. One of my little brothers stands in front of my mother. This occurred a lot in photos with her, and photos of her mother, too. I'd do it myself. Put someone in front of you to mitigate how fat you looked, a sort of trompe l'oeil with your size. I'm sitting on a step hunched over and clasping my knees to my chest to try and look smaller. I'm about 16, my hair is long and yellow and I'm wearing thick wire-rimmed aviator glasses and pink and yellow plaid pants that I felt so *normal* in, because the elephant bells were so very *au courant*.

My mother used other tricks to make herself more acceptable to the camera. She began to tilt chin upwards to minimize her turkey neck, all the loose, drapey skin from gaining and losing weight her whole life. Sometimes her chin is so far upwards it looks like she sees something on the ceiling. Then she adopted a method that was supposed to raise the corners of a drooping mouth: place the tip of your tongue against your palate and front teeth. There was always some way to mollify your existence, some way of having hat in hand for being unsightly.

We'd planned a new family photograph that spring, even though my mother had died three months earlier, and she'd kind of been the whole point of it. Nevertheless, my father, five kids and spouses, thirteen grandchildren, and a great-grandchild gathered in my sister's backyard on a bright summer day. It's taken me years to look at the pictures. The only one who is smiling and sunny is the six-month-old baby. The rest of us have foreheads wrinkled with distraction, and our faces are ruddy from the crying and fighting through raw sorrow. We tried to make our grimaces look like smiles: *Well, we're here, we don't know what t'hell we're doing but... we showed up.*

Somewhere my mother was probably relieved she got out of the whole clusterfuck.

Every Day
Richards, Elizabeth
8/10
Woman + her family take care of her ex-boyfriend
+ father of her oldest child who is dying from ALS.

A ustin seemed vaguely familiar when Alan and I got back after my mother's funeral. I stared out the car window as we drove home from the airport. We'd lived there almost eight years, but it was like looking at it through a threadbare sheet. The shapes of the city, the shapes of our life, were there, but I couldn't quite make sense of them. *Has this always been the way home from the airport? Has that gas station always been on that corner?* We pulled into the driveway. I had forgotten what an ugly green color the house was.

Pots and pans clanked in the kitchen as I started unpacking the suitcases. The oven beeped to preheat, then came the metallic shimmying sound of foil being torn off its roll. I peeked around the bedroom door and across the living room. Alan was making himself Shake N' Bake pork chops. Life went on, writ small with pork chops in a pre-packaged coating. I left the suitcase on the bed in situ, and dragged a ratty vinyl recliner we'd gotten off craigslist in front of the television. I watched movies for days, plunked a foot away from the screen, while Alan had to pass back and forth between the TV and me to get through the house. He never said a word, but he would reach out to rub my back or cup my cheek in his hand or hand me a pint of Ben and Jerry's. Movie after movie droned on, and I sat there wondering when my mother's death would be *over*, like it was a phase she was going through and all I needed to do was wait it out.

I felt like an out-of-sync animatronic figure in the months that followed. I was making the motions of living, but everything was just off. Constantly preoccupied, I observed myself: *This is how we grocery shop. This is doing laundry. I am walking the dog—people walk their dogs.* I had an odd sensation of my arms "watering," as if they could salivate, to embrace her again even though we'd never been much for hugging. Sometimes I felt like I could still hear her voice ringing in my ears, like a very specific tinnitus. I'd wake up crying in the mornings. The tears would slide down my temples into my hair, and the snot would roll right back into my nose. I began to dread even going to sleep at night. What was going on?

I looked up my feelings in the dictionary:

The verb "miss," as in "to miss someone," is a contranym, one word with two opposite meanings. "Missing" can mean to be either connected or disconnected. To miss people means to love them, to be partial to them, incomplete without them, and therefore missing the other part of what makes you whole.

To notice the absence or loss of: *When did you first miss your wallet?*
   3: to fail to obtain <ignorance *misses* the best things in this life
— W. R. Inge
   4: ESCAPE, AVOID <just *missed* hitting the other car
   6: to fail to comprehend, sense, or experience <*missed* the point of the speech

Gone
Gardner, Lisa
7.5/10
Missing woman (kidnapped) + later a child.

Songs for the Missing
O'Nan, S.
8 (7?)/10

Here On Earth
Hoffman, Alice
5/10
Woman + 15 year old daughter go back from West Coast to East Coast
for funeral. She falls back in love with high school beau. Leaves husband
+ stays with abusive man who has become rich. Very dumb woman who
puts daughter in jeopardy.

Viking Funeral
Stephen H. Cannell
Large print during eye problem

L ess than a month after my mother's funeral, I flew back to Minnesota for what would have been her 80th birthday. None of us knew what we should do on that day, but I'd be there for whatever it was. *One foot in front of the other,* she would have counseled.

One night I couldn't sleep, and I crept upstairs to the kitchen, as if my mother might have been there to yell from her bedroom with her bat-like hearing, "Who's in the kitchen? What are you doing in the kitchen?" As always, I started canvassing the cupboards and the refrigerator. I'd heard of people losing a lot of weight after a death, their sorrow crippling them to the point of not being able to get food into their mouth. I kind of hoped that would happen to me in my grief, and I know my mother would have approved.

I wasn't hungry (but maybe I *could* be if I tried hard enough and found the right thing). Going through the pantry and refrigerator was something I'd done my whole life, and I reverted to it every time I was back in my parents' house even if I was only there for 20 seconds. I swear if I were a firefighter running into a blazing house to save someone, I'd still crack open the freezer and slam through the cupboards looking for ice cream and ripple chips.

I sat at the dining room table to a stack of sympathy cards and notes, a good two inches high, and I was curious about the woman they described, a woman I kind of knew.

So many notes mentioned how easy my mother was to talk to. Her frankness. Perceptivity. Humor—note after note about my mother's sense of humor. My father is good-humored and enjoys a good joke. But my mother was *funny*: sly. Acerbic. Droll. Never letting on if she was just trying to get a reaction out of someone for her own amusement or letting people think she was just callin' 'em like she saw 'em.

We were watching the results of the Twin Cities marathon on television. It was the first year of the wheelchair division and when the sportscaster announced the winner, my mother said, "Big deal. They get to ride the whole way."

When she had to have a hysterectomy, my brother went to visit her in the hospital. In his early twenties and still trying to figure out his life, he'd lived in some shabby rooming houses and apartments along the way. He teased my mother: "You got rid of the first place I lived!" She replied through a painkiller haze, "The *nicest* place you've ever lived."

I always wanted the details when my mother went to a funeral. Maybe it was someone I knew peripherally or someone she'd talked about. I wanted to know who'd come, if anyone who shared memories during the service said something shocking, and how the food was. "How was the funeral?" I'd ask. Every single time, my mother would reply with sarcastic pleasantness, "It was really fun!"

And then with a flutter of her eyes: *"Howthehelldoyouthinkitwas?! Honestly, M.J.!"*

After Alan and I got married at the justice of the peace, we had a family picnic at my parents' house. My mother arranged everything buffet-style on tables fashioned from sawhorses and lumber from my father's shop, and she helped ladle stuff on people's plates as they moved through the line. I watched her serve up huge helpings of her prized baked beans to everyone in front of me. When it was my turn, she tapped a tiny dab on my plate.

"It is your wedding night after all," she said, not even cracking a grin as she moved on to the next person in line with an overloaded ladle.

Big Trouble
Dave Barry
8/10
Similar to Hiaason type mystery. Also set in Miami.
Russian theft of nuclear weapon & selling of it.
Very funny– lots of nasty, weird and good guys.

Hold Tight
Harlan Coben
8/10
Always enjoy his books, page turner.

Seven Up - 8 + To The Nines
Evanovitch, Janet
7/10
Humorous bounty hunter book grandma kidnapped.
Stephanie Plum works for her looney cousin bail bondsman, Vinnie

Simple Truth
D. Baldacci
8/10
Can't remember but know I enjoyed it.

I n the weeks after my mother's death and sorting through closets and desk drawers, my father began finding random envelopes of cash. My mother made money here and there from garage sales she'd held over the years, or clothes or furniture she sold on consignment, and she hid it throughout the house. My father, an accountant to the last, said with a laugh of astonishment that the money totalled almost what the cremation and funeral had cost. Pragmatic to the last, maybe it was the rainy day she'd intended for her secret stash.

Blood Money
Perry, Thomas
7/10
Series with Jane (part Indian) who helps people disappear.
This one involves Mafia + lots of money.

The Winner
David Baldacci
6/10
Fixed lottery–winner a young woman who is forced to leave country with her baby due to possible murder charge.

Y our mother always had a hundred-dollar bill hidden in her wallet," Edna said.

Edna is one of my mother's oldest friends, and when I visit we always end up talking about my mother. She sits small in a cushy chair and adjusts her thick, enormous, pink-framed eyeglasses. My mother's friends knew her in a way I never could, and it's kind of a way of retracing my footsteps, looking for all the things I missed that were right in front of me when she was alive. A lifelong Lutheran, Edna is a person of deep faith, and she assures me that my mother and I will see each other again in heaven someday. I have my doubts about an afterlife, but it's comforting that someone else can hold that hope for me. Still, I better have my own room because my mother and I will drive each other crazy. I can see her furnishing the great beyond with a bunch of stuff that I don't want, but it'll turn out I need some of it, and my mother will have a little *I told you so* turn to her lips.

I was flummoxed. "A hundred dollars in her wallet? Really? Why?"

"She'd have money for a hotel in case she ever wanted to leave your father."

Surely my mother had her own credit card. Do hotels take cash anymore? If you could even find a decent hotel for that amount. Maybe a single one-hundred dollar bill was a talisman of options. She could still join the Ice Capades or hop a freight train or whatever my mother's idea might have been about the road not taken

—*if she wanted.* I think about that Benjamin in her wallet in her dying days, as she became weaker and weaker and would have needed my father's help to leave him.

The Summons
Grisham, John
7/10
Father of a judge dies + leaves over three million in cash. 2 sons trying to discover where it came from. Not as good as his others but did keep me interested.

God Save The Mark
Westlake, Donald
6/10
Fred is a con man's dream. Inherits $300,000 + tries to hang onto it.

I told Liz about the one-hundred dollar bill. Over the years, we siblings kind of recalibrate our recollections. The memories have been played over and over again so many times in our heads, they've started to warp. We try to get our bearings: *What house were we living in? Was that before or after they owned the liquor store?* We might be asking, *What did I miss? What don't I understand that I didn't even know I didn't understand and want to now?*

Liz nodded. "She also had a bag packed and hidden in the closet - just in case she needed it. Dad never knew about it." I stare at her, slack jawed. It occurs to me: "Was… she going to take us kids?"

She hesitated. "I...don't think so."

We looked at each other and laughed. We were older now--our own heartbreaks, marriages, and child-rearing and life under our belts. We didn't take it personally, survival and all.

Sometimes I asked my mother if she and my father had ever thought about divorce.

My father's zest for life could drive her crazy. His whole life, my father has gotten up every morning with zeal for a new day. He whistles in the bathroom during his ablutions, and cheerfully yells out news items he's hearing on the radio to my mother in the kitchen. Everything comes to a screeching halt when he rinses his mouth out after brushing his teeth. It is a loud, hawking up-from-the-back-of the throat noise, followed by a guttural cough and spit.

If you happened to be in the kitchen with my mother at the time, and hearing the goings-on down the hall, my mother would give a half-laugh and a half eye roll. "Every morning. Every morning for 55 years."

"Of course!" she said with a little puff. "Never seriously. Neither of us thought we could handle all you kids by ourselves."

Once I found a birthday card my mother had given my father. She wrote, *"I married 'up'. I can't imagine my life without you. I love you."*

Hitler's Niece
Hansen, Ron
Supposed to be his only true love. Did not finish.

Girl Who loved Tom Gordon
King, Stephen
Lost in woods, girl relies on baseball pitcher (T.G.) to get her through.

W hat do we think about our parents dating?"

Liz and I had bumped into a family friend at a local mall. We'd all grown up in the same neighborhood, and our families had been entwined ever since. After my mother died, his mother, a widow in her late 70s, and my father hung out together a lot, going to movies and concerts, and lunches and dinners with mutual friends.

My blood ran cold when Steve asked the question, and I gulped hard and tried to play it cool. His mother was lovely and serene, and we adored her. But she was, as Therese pointed out, my mother's worst nightmare: tall, slim, and long-legged. Worse - earnest and sweet-natured.

When I got home, I practically regurgitated the incident on Alan.

"*Dating!*" I keened.

"M.J.," he said, "Life goes on."

"I know - but does it have to go on *right now?*"

"Wouldn't your Mom want your Dad to be happy?"

I cried harder. "No!" I started laughing. "No, she wouldn't!"

Man + Wife
Klavan, Andrew
7/10
Strange book. Psychiatrist in happy marriage.
Wife shoots + kills a man from her past.

I could barely stand to glance in my parents' bedroom after my mother's death. The comforter on my mother's side of the bed stayed smooth and untouched, even after a night of my father tossing and turning on his side. He began putting a rose in a vase on her nightstand on her birthday and their wedding anniversary. When the mechanisms broke and the mattresses became compressed and lumpy a few years later, my father dismantled the whole thing and dragged it to the garage to sell on Craigslist. The new, merely queen-size bed seemed tiny and insubstantial in the room. I thought about asking him if he'd cried, or if it was just a fact of life, the way that the world kept spinning and the old things wore out and new things were needed. But I didn't want to know.

Devil's Bed
Krueger, Wm Kent
8/10
Myst. action – Secret Service agent Bo Thorson discovers a subversive group silently trying to take over government.

Sleeping Doll
Jeffrey Deaver
7/10
Many twists + turns but got long.

Sleep Tight
Frasier, Anne
7/10
Serial murders–two sisters–one FBI and one MPLS police.

My father burrowed into his workshop after my mother died. Our houses had always smelled of varnish and freshly cut wood, and my father often billowed sawdust wherever he walked. I'd grown up with the muffled sounds of a screeching bandsaw or the whine of a belt sander reverberating through the house.

The workshop in this house was grand. It had been a tuck-under garage in the back of the house, and the previous owner installed French doors which opened out to the backyard and a small creek at the bottom of a slope. My father put in floors salvaged from an old high-school basketball court, and one of his greatest finds was an old hospital gurney he found at Goodwill that he used as a work surface. It could be raised, lowered, or tilted for whatever needed to be done with a project. The walls were an intricate mosaic of tools and gadgets hung on pegboard. My father always knew where everything was: he could sense from afar if something was amiss in the workshop, if someone had borrowed a screwdriver or measuring tape without his knowledge. A small anteroom was stacked floor to ceiling with lumber for future projects, in all shapes and sizes and varieties, and organized by length.

My father can figure out how to build anything and fix anything. When my mother had her heart attack, we joked that all he'd need to replace the stent was a piece of maple, a bandsaw, and a Phillips screwdriver. We teased him that wood was his one true love, and he was only making do with Mom until marriage to lumber was legalized. Once I asked him why he didn't just move his bed down into his workshop. "You could be closer to your wood," I offered.

"The bed wouldn't fit down there." He thought. "Maybe a smaller bed would work.

I think he seriously considered it.

I t had been kind of a hobby for my parents to move houses. I think my mother got bored living in the same place, and my father always wanted a project, always wanting to be building or remodeling something, *anything*. The post-war crackerbox house was the first house, then a rambler, then a more modern house with a sunken living room on the tiny lake where we swam as kids. But never a split-level. My mother deeply resented split-levels. She didn't want to be forced to make a decision the minute she walked in the door, up or down. *No house is going to tell me what to do*, she'd say between set lips.

House of Sand And Fog
Andre Dubus
5/10
Iranian family buy a CA house at auction. It was a mistaken foreclosure.
Story of fight between woman who (owns?) + Iranian. Downer but
recommended by Marlene.

Beach House
Green, Jane
Started out with promise.
Turned dumb dumb dumb about ½ way through.

A Painted House
Grisham, John
9/10
Non-mystery – boy growing up in Arkansas on a poor cotton farm with
parents + grandparents. Very good.

Home Fires Burning
Inman, Robert
6/10
Nice story about small town during WWII. Got a bit long but enjoyable.

Blackbird House
Hoffman, Alice
8/10
Short book of many different people living at different times in a house on Cape Cod.

Secret Life of Bees
Kidd, Sue Monk
9/10
Girl in South Carolina runs away from home (1964) with a black nanny.

The Beach House
Patterson, James
9/10
Very rich influential in the Hamptons murder a young man + their wealth keeps them out of jail.
Attorney brother of murder vic sets up a forced trial. Usually do not like this author but book kept me interested – finished in 2 days.

Alan and I sat on an old mattress on the curb waiting for the *Got Junk* truck. We were moving back to Minnesota. My mother had died despite our efforts, and I wasn't going to make the same mistake with my father. Just as soon as the truck came for the last of the odds and ends, we'd get in the car and drive away. My sisters texted me that morning: "Wake up, wake up, today is the day they give babies away!"

I loved our Austin house, even if it was an ugly green that I'd never gotten around to repainting. The street name had been a huge selling point for me: Bill Hickcock Pass. So Texan, and spelled so wrong. The backyard was fenced in for Seymour, and I hung laundry on a clothesline outside. In the crackling sun even heavy Levis would be dry in 20 minutes, and folding them was like breaking down a cardboard box.

My parents visited us a couple of times, making do on a queen-size bed instead of the bendy beds at home. On one of their trips, my father and Alan replaced the dilapidated deck. My mother and I frequented all the Goodwills, swam in Barton Springs, and made dinner for the menfolk every night. My mother had examined the house, just like she'd done every place I lived, much like she was wont to inspect my siblings' brand new babies, unswaddling them and reswaddling them. She moved a chair by a window for Seymour. *Dogs like to look out the window. Didn't you know that?* My mother knew how much Alan loved meat of any sort, and one night she put leftover spaghetti in a casserole dish, and piled discs of breakfast sausages high atop it, teetering so high it was like processed pork Jenga. Alan was delighted and my mother was pleased.

We washed the dishes that night and she aimed the faucet nozzle at me and pressed the little black rubber button. "Did you know you had this?" she asked as she squirted water at me. How did she know I didn't know there was a sprayer? How did she know I'd been so aggravated, after all the money we'd spent buying a house? I had no idea what the button on the nozzle was for and I'd been afraid to press it for fear I'd ruin the house we'd just bought. But she knew.

The truck came and took away the last of our lives in Austin, and Alan, Seymour, and I stuffed ourselves in the packed Honda Civic and said nothing as we backed out of the driveway, and I looked away. It was the last home my mother would ever be in, the last house my mother would appraise corner to corner, the last time she'd tell me how things worked.

D riving down the main thoroughfare of the splayed suburb where Alan and I now lived and where my parents lived, everything reminded me of my mother. Peppered with fast-food restaurants, disheveled auto-repair shops, and vacated blocky buildings with enormous "For Lease" signs in front, I see "her" Culvers, "her" Goodwill, and Bob's Produce Ranch, a small grocery store. She liked to name-drop that she and my father knew Bob personally. On this roadway, a causeway runs over a small lake, a stretch of road I've driven a million times. There's a small municipal beach on the other side of the lake, and I have a memory of one of my mother's memories. Years ago she'd spent the day there with my sister and her three little kids. My mother sat in the sand with the youngest, a nine-month-old at the time, while my sister swam with the older two. He died in an accident a few months later. "I never don't think of Thomas when I see the beach," she'd say every time we drove that road.

Her Target store. I thought I'd never step foot in a Target store again, as if it might trigger another phone call with another misfortune. But what am I, nuts? My mother would have scoffed: *Life goes on, M.J.* So I tell myself I'm honoring her memory and her library, where I go now, and where I've amassed almost 400 books on my reading list. She rarely bought books. I pass through the rows and rows of books, and I wonder which ones she might have pulled off the shelf to read the back cover or flip it open and scan the pages.

n't think of her walking through the aisles surrounded
by the towers of all sorts of books, any of them a possibility for my
mother. I wanted to ask the long-time librarian if my mother had
ever had any overdue books, but it's unlikely. She considered it a
civic duty to return books on time.

Lily White
Isaacs, Susan
3 on scale of 1-5
*Long Island criminal defense lawyer. Con man Norman and his girl-
friend Mary Dean (??)... Lily's (her) sister takes her husband.*

These Granite Islands
Stonich, Sarah
Read 76 pages and could not get interested. Quit.

King of Torts
Grisham, John
6/10
*Becomes a class action (tort) attorney following 5 years as public defend-
er. Greed gets the best of him.*

Dark Lady
Patterson, Richard North
*Skullduggery of the building of a new stadium.
Four strange murders solved by woman DA.*

Master Butchers Singing Club
Erdrich, Louise
9/10
*Following WW1-butcher and his family move to America from Ger-
many (North Dakota) spans both wars. Excellent.*

Y ou look just like your mother from behind," my aunt Susan exclaimed.

It was my nephew's high school graduation party, and I'd just come back from refilling my plate at the sprawling, multi-station buffet. It was the kind of bacchanalia typical of my family. "Now this is just overkill," my mother would have said reproachfully, all the while filling her plate. Aunts and uncles and cousins and family friends swarmed the garage and driveway, many of whom I hadn't seen since my mother's funeral. I sat down with my aunt and my mother's friend Edna, who'd watched me at the buffet.

"Except for your height and the blonde hair, we could have sworn it was your mother!" Edna chimed in.

That can only mean one thing. I am blond, fair, and almost a foot taller than my mother, and we have the same body shape, the same "from behind." At one point, I might have been considered "Rubenesque," but middle-age arrived, and repeated losing and gaining weight had made my tummy a kind of graduated undulation of flesh, like a Fisher-Price stacking ring toy. Yet somehow, in keeping with our family butt heritage, my ass still managed to be flat and square. And weird. Like the crack didn't go all the way to the top, like it gave up trying to go all the way up, and flesh around my middle became a cornice on the other side at the top of my butt.

My mother's form.

I took a deep breath. It was hard to hear my mother mentioned, and I always hated people commenting on my appearance, good, bad, or however I would interpret that remark. I'd learned to joke about myself before anyone else could. Just like my mother had about herself, disarming people and getting a jump on the comments and judgments.

But the women's faces were earnest and tender. I studied a forkful of food not knowing what to say. My ass had brought back warm memories of someone they had loved dearly. Examining the tater-tot hot dish closely, it hit me. What exactly was so wrong about my mother's body? She'd spent her whole life trying to make it be something else, but she'd lived and breathed and moved and laughed and grieved and thought thoughts in that skin. That body birthed five babies, supported a family, owned businesses, got a realtor's license in her fifties. This human had quit the gym because of their discrimination policies against gays. She'd volunteered on the local Barack Obama campaign, doing the worst job possible given her considering her misanthropic streak: cold calling. To say nothing of arms expertly wielding a yardstick in self-defense and vacuuming the hell out of a house. . That body had taken her to damn near every Goodwill in the Twin Cities metro area *and* Austin. That body, that woman, that person endured surgeries and procedures and heart attacks and came out swinging, for crying out loud, in that amalgamation of flesh and bones and blood and corpuscles. My mother was the best water-treader in her water aerobics class, and I bet she could take on all comers.

Had my mother ever stopped to marvel at the sheer miracle of herself? Had she ever enjoyed herself in her skin? Had she ever even relaxed in her body, instead of being ever vigilant about how it was supposed to be? In that moment, to ridicule myself was to ridicule my mother. I balanced my paper plate on my lap and smiled weakly. "Oh… really?" I squeaked out. I took another bite of tater tot hot dish and relished it. Maybe I could make peace with it - and my mother - by just shutting up.

Body of Evidence
Patricia Cornwell

Everybody Loves Somebody
Scott, JoAnna
Short stories-got bored; quit half way

Some books really stuck in mother's craw, and she'd bring them up out of nowhere, apropos of nothing, possibly to exorcise them.

> Degarcy, David   1-04
> Last Things
>   Page 4 used the
> word eschatological –
> Made me angry at author
> so quit the book

Jackdaws
Follett, Ken
0/10
Read 45 pages and it started out like a romance – heroine named Flick.

Patterson, James
Four women (close friends) 1 chief of detectives solve murder in SF. Really quite dumb. From now on the first time author mentions "nibbling on her salad" the book is out of here. Don't plan to read any more by him.

Like the Cheesecake Incident. It'd been almost 40 years, and she still managed to shoehorn it into some random conversation. It was never a discussion, just a statement. *You know, when you ate all the cheesecake.* I was angry that she'd profiled me. After all, I was the fat one in the family. You'd think with all the crime and mystery novels she'd read, she would have known to at least interrogate me, due process and all that. My jaw would set and I'd think, "I didn't do it. And even if I did, it wasn't *all* of it - it was only about 1/32nd of the pan. IF it was me."

I was not going to give my mother the satisfaction of thinking she knew me.

S omewhere in that year we didn't know would be the last, my mother said to me, "You get me."

I don't remember if it was white or green outside, if it was winter or summer, a way of bisecting a Minnesota year to organize memories. The two of us sat in the TV room, watching some show, and my mother was snuggled low in a recliner with a comforter pulled up to her chin. She was getting smaller under the blankets and got cold even more easily those days. *You get me.* My mother said it more to the television than to me. It was easier that way.

I was surprised. I'm sure I took umbrage, but I didn't say anything. It was like saying I was like her, and I'd spent my whole life trying not to be like her. I'd stopped officially dieting, defiant of the diet industry and our culture's beauty standards. I wasn't going to careen from one magical diet to another and obsess day in, day out, about what I was eating or not eating. I wasn't going to wear voluminous and nondescript black clothing to blend into the woodwork. I wouldn't wear ratty old robes around the house, and I most certainly wasn't going to own a vacuum cleaner with which I could vacuum angrily. I would at least have the self-respect to wear sweat pants and I wouldn't even own a vacuum cleaner. Anything not to be like her, the *her* I'd thought she was for so long.

I'd had a glimmer of understanding that apples don't fall far from their trees - I'd not fallen far from mine, and she'd not fallen far from hers. I "got her" in ways I didn't even know were happening, and so I couldn't rail against them like the way I'd start crying to hear her voice on the phone when I was depressed or sad or had some drama underway. There were times I was so agonizingly lonely and everyone and everything felt so far away, no matter where I might have been living at the time. She'd pick up the phone, and I couldn't control my voice. She knew instantly. *I'm sorry,* I'd say, *I just start crying when I hear your voice.* It's not like she would have stroked my hair and soothed me. She would have made her voice firm and asked about the weather. Don't dwell on it. Some people don't have legs.

She got cancer, I got middle-aged, and it reversed. I would answer her calls, and it was my mother who would inhale sharply trying to control the tears. A sniffle, and then she'd say, *Dammit - I always cry when I hear your voice.* But she'd try to brush it off. *Oh, I'm just having a crummy day!* Crummy - a word I hardly ever hear anymore, and when I do, I can only hear it in her voice.

We couldn't help getting each other. But it was hard to change my story about her. I can't remember how I responded to my mother. Maybe we both just stared at the commercials rolling by on the TV and tried not to look at each other so we wouldn't cry.

Larry's Party
Shields, Carol
8/10
Larry loves to build mazes (gardener).
A simple story about his mazes and the maze of his life.

Pines Polka (sic)
Landvik, Lorna
5/10
Small northern MN town story. Got a bit like a poor soap opera.

Four Blind Mice
Patterson, James
6/10
Alex Cross involved in Viet Nam past offense by US military.
Same old story – getting tired of these books.

Despite my resistance to people - and groups - and - well, pretty much *everything* - I began a 12-step program for food and eating. I was exhausted by my own preoccupation with eating/not eating and my body, and I'd started to understand a little better my mother's own ups and downs. I attended meetings sporadically and always begrudgingly, and I always made a stop for chocolate after the meetings. After a few years I managed to make it to Step 9: *Made direct amends to such people wherever possible, except when to do so would injure them or others.*

One by one I contacted people from my past and present. But I avoided my mother. I was waiting for her to get better before we talked about *deepest most innermost feelings.* Or I didn't want to pick at the scabs of the past. Then she died. *Pulled the rug right out from under us,* as she would have put it.

The 12-step literature stated that one could *write out your amends to someone who is no longer available, and read it to them as if they were alive.*

The letter became worn and frayed from being carried around in my purse for months. I couldn't decide when and where I should read it to my mother, wherever, whatever she might be. It needed to be someplace special, somewhere that embodied the essence of who my mother was, and I couldn't decide among a Goodwill, Culvers, or the Fridley library. Finally one day I sat on a stone bench under the trees just outside of the doors of the windowless building of the library and carefully opened the letter. I read it aloud softly, as people passed by on their way in and out, their arms loaded with books.

Dear Mom:

Hope you're not busy right now but just want to tell you how sorry I am. For so many things.

I'm sorry about the cheesecake. IF I ate it, I'm really sorry.

I stole money from the card shop when I worked there. I'm sorry.

I'm sorry for the fight we had about my job. We didn't speak for months, and I stopped at the house to pick up my mail once. I walked right back out of the house without saying a word. You ran after me. (At least that's how I remember it, but you were never much of a runner so that can't possibly be right.) You were almost in tears. You said, "I haven't told anyone about this." Our not speaking to one another. I may have said, "So?" I had no idea I could cause you pain.

I'm so sorry for never really hearing you or hearing your stories. I was impatient, self-involved, and only wanted to talk about my life. What could you possibly have to say? And now I have so many questions.

So much gratitude for your and Dad's sacrifices when you were hardly in a position to make them, so many that I know I've taken them for granted. College. Braces. Making sure we all knew how to swim. I only just found out you yourself didn't know how to swim. But you made us love the water.

Thank you for your great, sly, caustic sense of humor that I appreciated more and more as I grew older. Your amazing intelligence, which I never gave you credit for because you couldn't remember all my friends' names.

I'm sorry I've blamed you for my being fat. (Which maybe you didn't know so I probably shouldn't have brought it up.) But you always kind of knew everything, you could read me like a book and maybe that's what made me mad. You gave me so much more than genetics, but it was all I could see. I see more now, and I see differently.

I miss you so much. It's become a dull ache these days, and I move with it as best I can, like making do with persistent arthritis. I wonder if this is how you felt when your mother died, and I wish I'd thought to ask what it was like losing your own mother when you were only 24.

I am sorry with all my heart and soul and bones. Wherever you are, I hope you can forgive me.

We're all doing okay, I guess. Liz makes your cheesecake now, and I haven't had to move into anyone's basement.

I love you.

I signed it the way I'd always signed cards and letters to her:

Mary Jo Pehl

I don't know how many Mary Jos she might know, wherever she is.

Raymond + Hannah
Marche, Stephen
Did not read because it did not appeal – series of letters – long distance
romance.

Uncomfortably Close
Lily Brett
8/10
Sweet book about Jewish woman with a business of letter writing for
others – very successful.

My mother liked to declare some things her "all-time favorite." She'd give a little shiver of delight, recalling how much pleasure it had given her. I'd laugh. "You say that about almost everything!"

She laughed too. "I knowwwwww… but this really is my all time favorite—of all time!"

Beach Music
Pat Conroy
One of my all time favorites

Life of Pi
Martell, Yann
9/10
Indian boy (16) leaves India with family. Ship sinks he is only one to survive except for a 500 lb. tiger. 278 days on raft with tiger. Took about 100 pages to get hooked.

Kitchen Boy
Robert Alexander
10/10
Story of the last days of the Tsar and family.
Claiming that one daughter (Maria) survived. (fiction)

Deal Breaker
Harlan Coben
10/10
First Myron Bolitar novel.

Water For Elephants
Gruene, Sara
10/10
Traveling circus during the depression years.
One of the best books I've ever read.

A Thousand Splendid Suns
Hosseini, Khaled
Does not get any better than this. Afghanistan.

The Kite Runner
Hosseini, Khaled
10/10
Afghanistan – doesn't get much better.

Guernsey Literary & Potato Peel Pie Society
Schaffer, MA + Barrows, Anne
10/10
Book of letters concerning after effects of #2 war on Guernsey channel
islands. Near the top of my 10 or 15 best.

Dreaming Water
Tsukiyama, Gail
10/10
Asian/Italian girl suffers from Werner's Disease (old age), tearjerker.

The Reader
Schlink, Bernhard
9/10
Very interesting + short book about a 15 year old boy who becomes sexu-
ally involved with a 30+ woman. Year later as a law student in Ger-
many he attends a trial for school + finds her as the defendant accused of
war crimes during the Holocaust.

Angela's Ashes
McCourt, Frank
Ireland. Great.

Snow In August
Hammil, Pete
9/10
11 year old Irish Catholic boy and his relationship with
neighborhood rabbi 1945-49

My mother used a Kindle more and more, and the tangible, 3D bound paper volumes and visits to the library got fewer and farther between. The latest book noted in the box was November 2010.

Olive Kitteridge
Strout, Elizabeth
Stories weaving into each other – very good.

Yokota Officers Club
Sarah Bird
8/10
Story of military brats. Always moving –
family of 6 children stationed in Japan.
Good story.

There were so many *lasts* that we didn't even know were the lasts. The last of her hair. Her short black and gray hair started coming out in patches, then she just shaved the rest of it. She took to wearing colorful, funky hats and caps. *Just until it grows back*, she assured us. *Just til it grows in again,* we assured her.

The last time she drove a car, her driving had become a little erratic. Even at her tallest, she could barely see over the steering wheel, and aging made her even shorter, and illness made her unfocused. Liz took on the task of revoking her driving privileges. *It's only temporary*, my sister assured her. *Just 'til you get stronger.*

The last time she was downstairs in their house. She was too weak to get up and down the stairs to do laundry or tidy up. *I'll get back down there again one of these days,* she told us. One of these days.

I gotta vacuum that bathroom rug. We all wanted to believe her. Vacuuming again would be a very good sign.

The last thing I saw her wear. I'd come to dread our Sunday phone calls, and that last morning I paced around the house doing everything I could to avoid it. I'd press the phone against my ear really hard, thinking my mother's cadence or her breath would give me clues about her condition that day, as if I might be able to hear the cancer cells mutating or dying off.

Long Last
Harlan Coben
7
Not as good as usual, terrorist cell.

[Stones From The River]
Hegi, Ursula
7/10
Germans during + after as well as prior to WW2. Trudi is a dwarf.
Good until about the last 75 pages when it got long + a bit too preachy
or introspective.

Final Detail
(Harlan Coben?)
Could not get into it so I quit.

I called her on video chat that day. She was lethargic from the medication, and she nodded to everything with a wan smile. She must have been exhausted trying to keep up with our demands that she get better. "Well, you look good!" I said, overly enthusiastically. Suddenly I was saying something to her she'd always say to me. No matter what crisis or despair I was in the middle of, she'd offer, "Well, you look good!"

"You look good, Mom!" She was wearing a red sweatshirt with a flower applique on the chest. Her eclectic fashion choices had always been bright colors and wild prints, but she'd devolved into brown and gray sweatpants and sweatshirts. I took the red as a good sign. "Think about spring coming," I cheerleadered. February in Minnesota is endless, with its tenacious grayness and thuggish cold. But I was going to life-coach my mother to health and wellness. "Won't spring be great? You're going to be feeling so good when summer comes. You know how you love summers." Rah-fucking-rah rah rah, I went on.

She smiled weakly and said, "Okay." How I fought the impulse to say, "Well, I guess I better get going. Bye."

Later that day Therese went to my parents' house to help my mother wax or Nair her mustache, but could not wake her up from her nap. The paramedics ripped the red sweatshirt down the middle in an attempt to revive her. They got her alive just enough to get her to the hospital where I would see her for the last time.

I've read the cards over and over again since that day in the coffee shop. I feel like I should wear white gloves when I handle the cards, like an archivist. I fear the paper disintegrating and the ink dimming, and I still won't have any answers. Maybe the answers change. Maybe the questions change. Maybe what I was really searching for was a book my mother might have recommended on how to live our lives after her death. Some sort of instruction manual for navigating the world, as if I might have been 14 and left with my younger brothers. *No friends in the house, stay out of the kitchen, no watching Love American Style.*

I've been able to make some sense, I think, of smudged ink or cryptic notes. Maybe there's a secret message embedded in all the index cards, some sort of communique for my eyes only. A code of random words underscored or certain letters capitalized, spelling out something like, "You were always my favorite."

Or "You are beautiful exactly as you are."

Maybe, "It's okay about the cheesecake. I mean, it is really good!"

"I get you."

Still, the cards make me laugh, and sometimes I cry. I get mad, too. I think, *Why did you even have us if you were just going to die?*

T he very last card in the box is out of alphabetical order and at the very tail end of the hundreds of others.

> Pehl, Mary Jo   8-04
> I lived with my Parents
> + other tales of terror
>
> 10 out 10

My feeble attempt at writing a book many years ago. It was a collection of short essays about moving back in with my parents at the age of 40 and then moving to New York. A small, niche publisher of graphic novels who'd been a fan of *Mystery Science Theater 3000* asked me if I'd write a book. This was all the proof I longed for that I was in fact *a writer, An Actual Writer.* Not just a transcriber of pop-song lyrics.

I thought it would be so easy. I mean, I had so many thoughts and words and ideas in my head, didn't I? I dashed it off in a matter of months, and the end result was embarrassing and amateurish - and very very slight. The cover illustration was garish and cartoony. Bad cartoony. The publisher had had to enlarge the font to make it appear somewhat more than a glorified pamphlet riddled with typos. In fact, in the first printing, my name was misspelled. When I pointed it out to the publisher, he exclaimed, "But we fact-checked it!"

He suggested a book tour. Via Greyhound bus. That summer, Greyhound was offering a $98 unlimited travel pass through the continental United States, which the publisher offered to purchase.

I was mortified by the whole thing. I pretended the "book" didn't exist. I stopped its publication and bought up copies so it wouldn't be out there for all the world to see, all the tens and tens of readers who might have been remotely interested. But somehow my mother had gotten her hands on a copy. It couldn't have taken her more than 20 minutes to read it, and yet, it got a card in the box. And a ten out of ten.

A brand new season of *Survivor* began a few weeks after Alan and I landed in Minnesota. My parents watched plenty of television, but it seemed like *Survivor* night would be especially lonely for my father. Jim and I decided we'd started watching it with him on Wednesday nights. We packed ourselves into the TV room for the 29th season premiere, *Survivor: San Juan Del Sur.* My father, Jim, Alan, Seymour, I, and assorted grandchildren yelled dibs on the recliners, and the rest relegated to folding chairs or pillows on the floor.

It's six years of our mid-week tradition, and with two new seasons every year, I've somehow managed to see twelve seasons. There's always a point where a family member visits the contestants, and they come running out of the bushes to surprise the contestant. I hate the show, but now I'm hooked and I try not to cry when I see mothers hug their kids. My family were staunch anti-huggers, but what I wouldn't give to bend over to my mother and squish her to me one more time.

Love In Present Tense
Hyde, Catherine Ryan
8/10
Very sweet book – man raises abandoned child.

Peony In Love
See, Lisa
Got much too long + detailed – had good reviews.

Tie That Binds
Haruf, Kent
7/10
Sad story of old woman + her hard life in the high plains of Colorado.
Mother dies young + she cares for nasty cruel old farmer father + her
brother. (read twice)

My mother's ashes are in a wooden urn in the living room, sitting on the gargantuan bureau. She is, in death as in life, adjacent to a recliner. My father made the urn, our very own Cash Bundren, and there are red "I voted" stickers all over it. My brother Mike affixed his sticker during the first election after my mother died. It's become a civic duty shrine to my mother, the rest of us following suit after every election since. Sometimes I still poke around the top drawer for the mirror and tweezers that I'm sure I've missed in the previous hundreds of times I've looked.

Next to the urn is a large black and white photograph of my mother on her wedding day. Her homemade wedding dress was modified from a Butterick pattern, the neckline raised and short sleeves lengthened for a church wedding in a small town. We found the dress when we cleaned out the closets, zipped up in a plastic garment bag and smooshed among all the clothes she was going to wear some day. There's no size tag on the dress and it seems really small. Had she been like brides everywhere and forever, trying to diet themselves to fit into their wedding dress?

In the picture, my mother sits with her legs tucked under her on the gray and white checkerboard linoleum floor of the church social hall. She is holding her bridal bouquet and the skirt of the dress is splayed in a big white circle around her with the brides-maids' bouquets arranged around the edge. My mother is looking slightly over her shoulder and upwards at the camera, as if the pho-tographer was on a chair for this vantage point. Her eyes are bright, her grin is broad and excited, like she feels beautiful, and you'd never know she'd always been self-conscious about her smile.

It was January, going on three years since my mother's death. It was dark outside, which could mean 4 p.m. or midnight, winters being what they are in Minnesota. My father has had back surgery, and we siblings were taking turns staying overnight with him during his recovery. It was my turn, and I sat in the living room in one of the recliners with a book on my lap while Alan was at home a few miles away with Seymour. My father walked in circles through the house with a walker, part of his rehabilitation therapy. He rounded past me in the recliner; then he went through the dining room, talking the whole time. I wore a loose, zip-front robe, a book on my lap, and my father's voice became muffled as he passed through the kitchen. The walker clanked on the tile in the foyer past the hat stand, like a tree of right angles and little hooks like tiny branches. It still held all of the hats that my mother wore when she lost her hair. My father can't bring himself to get rid of it.

I unconsciously run my fingers over my jawline and look at the books stacked on the coffee table, their covers dusty now. *The Boys in the Boat*, and *Fun Home*, a favorite of both my brother and me that he'd loaned her when she was up to reading again. The previous summer, I got my hair cropped very short and a little spikey, and my face has drooped enough to reveal cheekbones. I don't really look like my mother: my nose is too bulbous, my face too broad, and my skin tone so fair. But sometimes, in a mirror, I catch a glimpse of her.

Who am I now, without my mother to ricochet off of? The endless gives and takes as we kept being mother and daughter in the only way we knew how, in maybe the only way she knew how to be a daughter to her mother. I have this urge, this itch in my hands, to pick up a phone, call her, and tell her how agonizing her death has been to us. *We don't know what to do without you here to tell us that some people don't have legs. We're trying not to be downtrodden.*

I turned on the lamp next to the urn. She would have been secretly pleased to fit into such a small container. Photographs cycled through an electronic frame. Every couple of seconds, a picture dissolved into the next one, making my mother a mirage. Many of the things my mother had given me over the years have worn out or broken down. My memories feel like that too, like they are fraying every time I roll them over and over in my head.

I leaned back in the recliner as my father clomped by again. The first few pages of my book described in acute detail the slaughtering of a goat. My father talked about the wood he used for the hat rack. He told me about the roof gutters in the neighborhood - the Johnsons have Leafguard, but the Nelsons have Gutter Helmet - and he told me the year each was installed. I closed the book. *Author graphically depicts goat butchering, so I stopped.* I murmured some "Is that right?"s or "Oh, really!"s. It's the kind of chit-chat that used to drive me crazy with my mother. I didn't know she was really telling me about her life. So I listen. I try to listen. I don't want to miss a thing. The hat rack is made of oak.

Many thanks:

Beth Black
Ken Dahler
Alonso Duralde
Meleah Maynard
Steve Schirra
Emily Ziring
RAD
Accountabili-buddies Melinda Kordich and Pete Colburn

Patricia Houlihan and her class at the Loft Literary Center,
Shaping the Longer Work in Creative Nonfiction

Robert Canipe and Patty Thompson, Redhawk Publications

Anoka County Library, and libraries everywhere

Dot

ABOUT THE AUTHOR

Mary Jo Pehl is a writer and cast member on the twice Emmy-nominated and Peabody Awarding winning *Mystery Science Theater 3000*. She's been published in magazines, websites, and numerous anthologies, and her commentaries have been heard on NPR's *All Things Considered*. As a comedian and storyteller, Mary Jo has appeared on stages and at comedy festivals throughout the land, and lives in the Twin Cities.

Made in the USA
Monee, IL
24 April 2023